YVES SAINT LAURENT
FORM AND FASHION

YVES SAINT LAURENT
FORM AND FASHION

EDITORIAL DIRECTION BY ELSA JANSSEN

Flammarion

Musée Yves Saint Laurent Paris

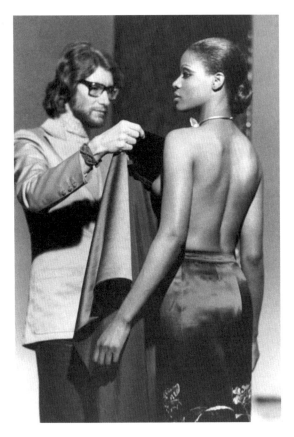
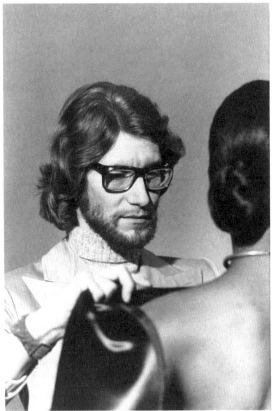

Yves Saint Laurent, Lisette Malidor, and Pierre Bergé
during preparations for the *Show Roland Petit*
television program, broadcast on January 2, 1971.
Photographs by Giancarlo Botti

As is true for any creative process as seen over centuries of artistic expression and across the globe whether in the field of fashion, architecture, interior or garden design, a work of art begins with a conceptual notion or idea. For Yves Saint Laurent, this process was often set in motion with a rough sketch, which the couturier would, at times, repeatedly rework until he was satisfied that his vision had been captured on paper.

This ongoing reworking of proportions and volumes was characteristic of the Frenchman's approach to design. It illustrates how Saint Laurent viewed his profession and the importance he placed on refining his craft in relationship to the constant flux of the world around him, which radically changed throughout his career.

Just as a painter might rework a canvas, adjusting light, color, filled or empty spaces; just as the painting could reflect contemporary social issues or perspectives, Yves Saint Laurent adhered repeatedly to the axiom first stated in a treatise by the influential late nineteenth-century American architect Louis Sullivan, that "form follows function." This concept of form being in the service of function, which in turn inspired early twentieth-century architecture, most notably the Bauhaus movement, had a longstanding influence on the French couturier: for him, an article of clothing inherently relates to its purpose or function.

The exhibition *Yves Saint Laurent: Shapes and Forms*, presented at the Musée Yves Saint Laurent Paris, cocurated by the museum's director, Elsa Janssen, and its head of collections, Serena Bucalo-Mussely, explores the way in which form and color are used as constructive elements within the rich vocabulary of the couturier's vast oeuvre.

Of special note is the enlightening dialogue the exhibition curators have engendered between some of the most iconic clothing constructions by Saint Laurent and works by the contemporary German artist Claudia Wieser, whose dramatic and vibrant artistic production is often inspired by, and integrated with, spatial and architectural expression. Wieser's majestic piece, a reflection on Le Corbusier's *Le Poème de l'angle droit* (The Poem of the Right Angle), reveals the artist's attention to proportion, volume, and form, as well as the salient importance to her of color. This dynamic, thought-provoking approach to Saint Laurent's work from a contemporary perspective is one that we encourage at the Fondation Pierre Bergé – Yves Saint Laurent.

On behalf of the entire board of directors of the Foundation, it is with great pride that I thank not only our invited artist and her co-curators, but also the scientific committee composed of Alice Coulon-Saillard, Domitille Éblé, and Judith Lamas, all members of the team at the Musée Yves Saint Laurent Paris. Their collective and combined efforts further illustrate the richness and unique hallmarks of the vast archives that constitute the Foundation's holdings.

May our visitors discover yet another rich aspect of the great French couturier's work, amid the myriad of pentimenti those stunning exploratory drawings that play such an important role in Saint Laurent's creative process and that underpin his influential repertoire.

MADISON COX
President, Fondation Pierre Bergé – Yves Saint Laurent

Yves Saint Laurent in his apartment
at 55 rue de Babylone, Paris, 1972.
Photograph by Henry Clarke, published in British *Vogue*

Through the exhibition *Gold*,[1] I enjoyed revealing the sunny and glamorous side of Yves Saint Laurent's work; with *Yves Saint Laurent: Shapes and Forms*, I have savored the pleasure of showing the abstract, modern, radical creator that he also was. Yves Saint Laurent still has surprises in store. Setting off to explore what he poetically called his "aesthetic spirits" carries with it the certainty of discovering within his work multiple layers of correspondence with the history of modern art and forms.

Yves Saint Laurent was a man of contrasts. Classic and modern, baroque and minimalist, a colorist and a master in the use of black, he concealed within his work an infinite number of possible interpretations. While his "homage" collections[2] are the aspects of his work that are most frequently cited, here we discover the work of an artist who was of his time, surrounded by his peers and influenced by the same breaks with the forms of the past. Art history has shown how, wherever they may live, artists are able to set up dialogues and maintain a closeness with each other; how all artists are inspired by references, myths, and observations of society that draw them to similar forms of expression and obsession.

The three chapters of *Form and Fashion*, "Minimalism," "Colors," and "Black and White," situate Yves Saint Laurent within the context of the history of art and form. With the three authors, Cécile Bargues, Serena Bucalo-Mussely, and Julien Fronsacq, it has been a huge pleasure to discover correspondence with Ellsworth Kelly, Sonia Delaunay, and Varvara Stepanova, to name only a few, in the work of Yves Saint Laurent. Three authors, three art historians, three theoreticians of form, together focused on the work of a great couturier.

At the Musée Yves Saint Laurent Paris our aim today is to set the work of Yves Saint Laurent in the context of the history of art, on the one hand offering an analysis of his imagination and creativity in the light of major artistic currents, and on the other exhibiting his work alongside that of contemporary artists.

This catalog is published to accompany the exhibition *Yves Saint Laurent: Shapes and Forms*, to which I also wanted to invite Claudia Wieser to contribute. The work of this German artist, born in 1973, positions her in a line of artists who flirt with the decorative arts. What do Yves Saint Laurent and Claudia Wieser have in common? A sense of harmony, certainly; a mastery of color, a simplicity of form, a love of materials. The exhibition was constructed around the points where the visions of these two artists intersect, with Claudia Wieser's works offering responses to the monochrome minimalism of Saint Laurent's jumpsuits, to the blocks of flat color of his dresses, and to the graphic effects of his black-and-white silhouettes. With her ceramic works, drawings on paper, wallpapers, and sculptures in wood, Claudia Wieser composes a total environment that molds itself to the architecture of the museum galleries. Readers of this catalog can admire a portfolio of her compositions created around Yves Saint Laurent accessories.

A "duo show" that shines a new light on the work of Yves Saint Laurent, on its modernity and its timelessness.

I offer my sincerest thanks, first and foremost, to the team at the Musée Yves Saint Laurent Paris who have helped in the preparation of this exhibition and catalog, as well as to all the other individuals who have been involved in this project: Claudia Wieser, of course, Cécile Bargues, Serena Bucalo-Mussely, and Julien Fronsacq for their immersive approach to the world of Yves Saint Laurent, and Valérie Weill and Matthieu Lavanchy for the photographs that illustrate this catalog. Finally, I would like to express my gratitude to Madison Cox for the confidence he has placed in us.

1. The exhibition *Gold by Yves Saint Laurent* took place at the Musée Yves Saint Laurent Paris from October 13, 2022 to May 13, 2023. The catalog was edited by Elsa Janssen and published by Gallimard.
2. Throughout his career Yves Saint Laurent dedicated collections to artists he admired, including Piet Mondrian (1872–1944), Pablo Picasso (1881–1973), and Henri Matisse (1869–1954).

ELSA JANSSEN
Director, Musée Yves Saint Laurent Paris

MINIMALISM

"My aim is to pare back as much as possible,
just as a painter pares back as much as possible
to perfect their style, just as a writer
questions everything, too. With every collection,
in fact, I question everything."

YVES SAINT LAURENT, 1987

Page 10:
Yves Saint Laurent and Sheila Bailie
during preparations for the spring–summer
1964 haute couture collection, in the studio
at 30 bis rue Spontini, Paris.
Photograph by Robert A. Freson

Ensemble of hats in velvet, wool, and felt,
autumn–winter haute couture collections,
1978, 1990, 1994, and 2001.
Photograph by Matthieu Lavanchy

SIMPLICITY
OF FORMS

CÉCILE BARGUES

"I want fashion that is extremely restrained," declared Yves Saint Laurent during the first runway show of the fashion house bearing his own name. "My setting will be as pared back as the fashions I am trying to launch."[1] He simplified. He lightened. "Stripping down" and "purity of construction,"[2] were his watchwords from the outset; his fashion was as simple as the "Trapeze" line from his first collection at Dior in January 1958 (pp. 18, 22–23), as simple as the furniture by designers such as Jean-Michel Frank and Eyre de Lanux that he would surround himself with, as simple as the art he loved. Despite the proliferation of styles and genres that he developed throughout his career, up to and including the most flamboyant of baroque, and despite the breadth of his choices, running right through the career and passions of Yves Saint Laurent there was nonetheless a clear line of restraint, absolute efficiency and economy of means. "The clothes were cut very close and highlighted only the lines of the body. There was nothing else: no decorations, no additions, nothing. It was just a line,"[3] he observed in 1975 (pp. 136–37).

"JUST A LINE"

Simple forms, blocks of solid color, tactile materials, precision of line and conception: Saint Laurent was to work out, in his own way, how to let the fabric speak and to distill everything to its quintessence. In the beginning, at Christian Dior, he designed dresses that hung from the shoulders, easier to wear than the cinched waists and corseted lines of the New Look that had garnered so much attention. Gradually, the flowing lines highlighted the verticality of the volumes, the movements of the body, the flexibility of the look: the dark navy, double-breasted I dress, wool ensembles, peacoats, and full coats ensured the freedom of movement that was essential for Saint Laurent, who saw clothes as a form of protection, or even, he would say, a home to live in. His white toile patterns and sketches for the "Trapeze" collection, pared back to the essence of the line, are almost like architectural models designed to be worn. His work with hats (Saint Laurent being one of the few couture houses to have its own in-house millinery studio) followed the same trajectory, using wooden forms that looked like small-scale abstract sculptures,

1. Yves Saint Laurent quoted by Laurence Benaïm in *Yves Saint Laurent*, rev. ed. (Paris: Le Livre de Poche, 2010), 195.
2. Program to the spring–summer 1958 collection by Yves Saint Laurent for Dior, introducing the "Trapeze" line.
3. Yves Saint Laurent quoted by Christian Geelhaar in "Mode-Kunst-Mode," *Tages-Anzeiger Magazin*, 20 December, 1975; see Mouna Mekouar, introduction to *Yves Saint Laurent aux musées* (Paris: Centre Pompidou – Musée national d'art moderne / Musée du Louvre / Musée d'Orsay / Musée national Picasso-Paris / Musée Yves Saint Laurent Paris / Gallimard, 2022), 11.

and with designs ranging from the simplest of wide-brimmed elegance to the most startling of geometric shapes. The power of their effect lay in his research and a meticulous choice of the materials that would give the design life as a volume in space. This culture of materials, so to speak, set Saint Laurent apart from an aspect of modernism that had originally caught his attention, including the machinism specific to Le Corbusier, some of whose furniture designs with Pierre Jeanneret and Charlotte Perriand he owned in reissued editions (p. 15).

SAINT LAURENT AND FRANK, *"L'ÉTRANGE LUXE DU RIEN"*

From that point on, many of Saint Laurent's designs appeared to bear comparison to or to conspire in spirit with the famously minimalist interiors of Jean-Michel Frank, like another expression of equilibrium, of a boundless technical mastery of volumes and lines, and all achieved with flawless insouciance and even a certain modesty. Convinced that we live and even dream better when less hemmed in and cluttered, both Saint Laurent and Frank created space for the individual, for movements of the body, for the wanderings of the mind. In the words of François Mauriac, they created *"l'étrange luxe du rien"*[4] or "the curious luxury of absence." And with this particular notion of comfort—in other words of stripping away everything that weighs you down and strews obstacles in your path. It was the geometrical fullness of an enveloping "Trapeze" coat. It was the hieratic, monolithic quality of the Comfortable club armchair, protecting and insulating the user. Saint Laurent navigated a way between the most elaborately worked fabrics, tweeds formerly reserved for men's suits, and ordinary jersey, while Frank hijacked materials and turned them to new uses. His apartments were sparsely furnished with tables in straw marquetry or mica, armoires with gypsum panels and a few rare *objets*, while he covered seats with burlap, then otherwise used as sacking,

and wove rugs from raffia. There is a great deal to be said about this aesthetic of contrasts, and even about the contradictions that inspired both artists. Far more than merely a couturier or an interior decorator, both were radical and irreverent in their work, even if the passage of time and its gradual absorption into popular culture have tended to soften the astringent qualities of these bold new departures. Pierre Bergé and Yves Saint Laurent were possibly the earliest connoisseurs and collectors of Frank's work, and were pioneers of our contemporary infatuation with Marie-Laure and Charles de Noailles, whose Paris townhouse, partly designed by Frank around 1925 and with its salon walls skillfully lined with parchment, had such a profound effect on them. By then Frank had fallen into obscurity, and many of his interiors had been lost, destroyed, or covered up, even before his death by suicide in New York in 1941. What an astonishing revelation it must have been— as well as the beginning of a long series of half-coincidences. Saint Laurent adored Proust; so did Frank. They were separated by thirty years, yet their affinities, admirations, and friendships overlapped, embracing Louis Aragon, for whom Frank had designed an apartment in the early 1920s, as he had for Nancy Cunard (p. 15); the surrealist writer René Crevel, his friend from his teenage years; and the brothers Diego and Alberto Giacometti, who designed furniture, lamps, bowls, and sometimes fireplaces for him. Hence the simplicity that informed Saint Laurent's work was also the product and extension of all these enthusiasms combined.

THE COLLECTION AS POINT OF REFERENCE

In Marie-Laure de Noailles's hôtel particulier on place des États-Unis, Saint Laurent had seen the collection—extremely rare in both scope

4.   François Mauriac quoted by Pierre-Emmanuel Martin-Vivier in *Jean-Michel Frank. L'étrange luxe du rien* (Paris: Norma, 2006); and *Jean-Michel Frank. Un décorateur dans le Paris des années 30* (Paris: Fondation Pierre Bergé – Yves Saint Laurent / Norma, 2009).

Above:
Salon of Nancy Cunard's apartment
with decorations by Jean-Michel Frank,
Paris, c.1924

Yves Saint Laurent on a chaise longue
designed by Charlotte Perriand
for Le Corbusier, in his apartment
at 55 rue de Babylone, Paris, 1983.
Photograph by Duane Michals

Yves Saint Laurent in his apartment at 3 place Vauban.
Behind him are a Senufo bird from the Ivory Coast
(late nineteenth century) and a floor lamp
by Isamu Noguchi, Paris, 1967.
Photograph by Henri Elwing, published in *Elle*

and quality—that she had assembled with her husband (and that in Frank's opinion cluttered the space horribly, an ambivalence that could also be observed in the decoration of the duplex on rue de Babylone). The collection was to serve as his model for the principle of demolishing boundaries between different periods and artistic styles, and even different tastes. The now famous collection that Yves Saint Laurent forged with Pierre Bergé began in 1960 with a large Senufo bird (p. 16), followed by a sculpture in wood by Constantin Brancusi, *Portrait of Madame L.R.* (right); later came three paintings by Piet Mondrian (p. 116), and finally a ready-made by Marcel Duchamp (*Belle Haleine, Eau de Voilette*).[5] The simplicity of African art; its echoes in Brancusi's sculpture and especially his *Birds*, whose purity and élan Saint Laurent would muse upon in his work; the absolute qualities of neoplasticism; the revolution in identities and categories in Dadaism; and Duchamp, who for Pierre Bergé was "the greatest artist of the twentieth century … for all sorts of reasons: because he destabilized the very history of painting, because he was an artist who simultaneously made all things possible and all things impossible":[6] could a clearer manifesto be hoped for? In a collection that grew to an enormous size over the years we could pick out names such as Frans Hals, Théodore Géricault, and Francisco de Goya, alongside Fernand Léger, Pablo Picasso, Paul Klee, and Giorgio de Chirico, and still be no nearer offering a comprehensive idea of the treasures it contained. All of these artists were like compass bearings, accompanying Saint Laurent on his explorations.

When Saint Laurent's tastes and inclinations started to take shape, mainly in the early 1960s, before becoming more definite, they quite often ran counter to the officially sanctioned tastes and hierarchies of the Paris art market and museums; the most conspicuous example of this related to Mondrian, whose first retrospective in a French museum was held in 1969, while his first painting did not enter the French national collections until

1975. Saint Laurent observed that his "Homage to Mondrian" dresses (1965, p. 63), which did not reference any specific neoplastic composition but set out to transpose a utopian version to fashion, "helped to make known to the general public an immense and forgotten artist, who in my opinion approached purity more closely than other artist in the twentieth century."[7]

5.   As described by Yves Saint Laurent in an interview published in *Air France Madame*, August–September 1990: "'What was the first painting you bought?' 'The first "real" painting was a Mondrian.' 'And what was the last?' 'Marcel Duchamp.'" He also spoke elsewhere about the Senufo bird and the Brancusi.
6.   Interview with Pierre Bergé by Laure Adler, *Pierre Bergé, Yves Saint Laurent. Histoire de notre collection de tableaux* (Arles: Actes Sud, 2009).
7.   See Bernard Blistène, "Une œuvre d'art peut-elle en cacher une autre ? Les exercices d'admiration d'Yves Saint Laurent," *Yves Saint Laurent* (Paris: Petit Palais / Éditions de la Martinière, 2010), 310.

Constantin Brancusi, *Madame L.R.*
(*Portrait de Madame L.R.*), 1914–17, carved oak, height 3 ft. 10⅛ in. (117.1 cm), former collection of Yves Saint Laurent and Pierre Bergé

In 1965, long before he was in a position to acquire any of his paintings, Saint Laurent knew Mondrian's work mainly from books, notably Michel Seuphor's monograph published in 1956. A voracious reader, Saint Laurent virtually lived in his library, which grew to thousands of volumes, finding sustenance in images from every period and continent, in a world of reproductions that he called his *"réserve"* and consulted daily, and of which he used to say: "This is where I make my most wonderful voyages."[8] This—at least as much as in his collection of art—was where he most probably found his sources of inspiration.

THE SOVIET
AVANT-GARDE

In the geometric shapes and volumes verging on the exaggerated of some of Saint Laurent's designs, dresses, and ensembles, especially from the 1980s, as well as in their strong palette that went beyond primary colors, it is possible to see links with the constructivist work of Lyubov Popova and Varvara Stepanova (p. 18), who had pushed their designs for clothing in the early years of the USSR to considerable lengths. Stepanova, notably, designed a one-piece sports suit, unisex, loose-fitting, and short, which was to find distant echoes in some of Saint Laurent's jumpsuits. Did he know of it? Possibly, through a rather tenuous network of connections with the Russian avant-garde. A photograph shows him in Moscow with Andy Warhol and Lilya Brik, for whom he had immense respect. Saint Laurent had read everything that had been written about this woman. She had become a symbol of women's liberation after the October Revolution, muse of the poet Mayakovsky and sister of Elsa Triolet (who was married to Aragon), and whose widely published portrait had been painted by Varvara Stepanova's husband,

8. Yves Saint Laurent quoted in "Je suis un homme scandaleux, finalement—Yves Saint Laurent par Catherine Deneuve," *Globe*, January 1986.

Research sketch for the Christian Dior spring–summer 1958 haute couture collection by Yves Saint Laurent, pencil on paper, 12²/₃ × 4³/₄ in. (32 × 12.5 cm)

Alexander Rodchenko. Whatever the case, the roots of a garment as commonplace as today's jumpsuit run deep: sported by Rodchenko, László Moholy-Nagy, and Dada artists in Berlin, who wore workers' overalls to mark their "aversion to playing the artist," according to Raoul Hausmann,[9] this one-piece garment was adopted from the 1920s by the women in their circles, fearless and chafing at the roles in which society pigeonholed them.

The jumpsuit made its first appearance at Saint Laurent in the summer of 1968, and by the mid-1970s, in a shape that echoed loose-fitting workers' overalls, it was a huge success. In its own way and social milieu, it followed the changing position of women in a world that had undergone profound changes, echoing their determination to have control over their own bodies and to embrace freedom of movement, at a time when experiments from the past were gaining prominence once more and a forgotten aspect of the avant-garde was emerging into full relevance again. It was almost as though Saint Laurent's determined and complete simplicity had opened the way to his radicalism.

9.   Raoul Hausmann, "Peinture nouvelle et photomontage," *Courrier Dada* [1958], ed. Marc Dachy, rev. ed. (Paris: Allia, 2004), 42.

Varvara Stepanova, unisex sportswear, 1928.
Photograph by Alexander Rodchenko

Pages 20–21:
Models from the Christian Dior
autumn–winter 1958 haute couture collection
by Yves Saint Laurent, Saint-Cloud.
Photograph by Pierre Boulat

"Refrain" dress, Christian Dior
spring–summer 1958 haute couture
collection by Yves Saint Laurent, Paris.
Photograph by Willy Maywald

"Seduction" dress in shantung,
Christian Dior spring–summer 1958
haute couture collection by Yves Saint Laurent.
Photograph by Matthieu Lavanchy

MODERN LINES
AT DIOR

When Yves Saint Laurent became artistic
director of the House of Dior at the age
of twenty-one, following the death of
Christian Dior (1905–1957), he continued
Christian Dior's explorations of geometric cuts.
For spring–summer 1958, he designed
the "Trapeze" line, with flared, loose-fitting
shapes that lent freedom to the body.
The ensembles in the collection owed their
elegance to the simplicity and clean lines
of their construction. The show was a triumph.
Saint Laurent's success was assured and,
in his desire to respond to the needs of
a clientele that was "younger" than the
traditional target audience of haute couture,
he created lines that were more modern,
and more compatible with the practicalities
of life for a younger generation. The belted
shape and button front of the "Stockholm" dress
in thick beige wool give it a modernist look.
S. B.-M.

"Stockholm" dress in wool, Christian Dior
spring–summer 1959 haute couture
collection by Yves Saint Laurent.
Photograph by Matthieu Lavanchy

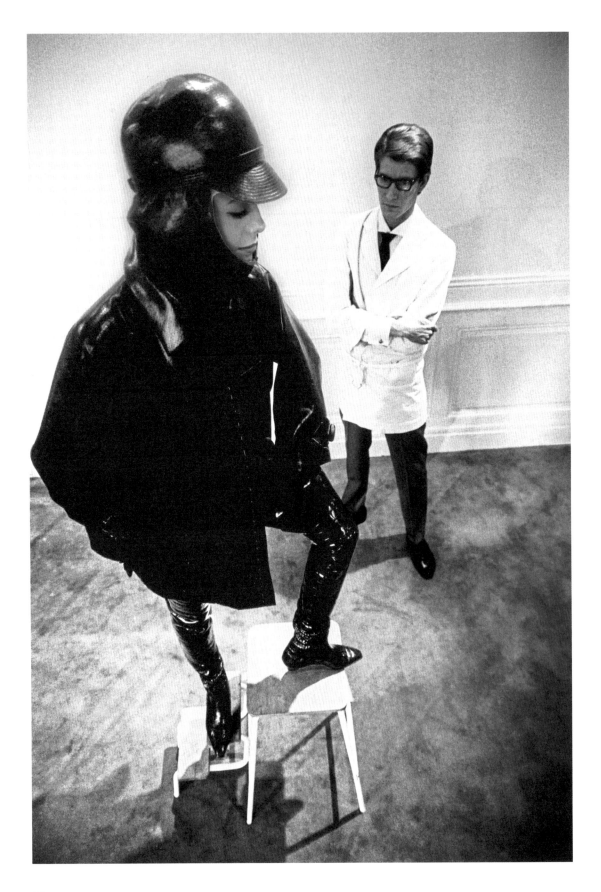

26

Paule de Mérindol wearing a sports ensemble
from the autumn–winter 1963 haute couture
collection and Yves Saint Laurent,
30 bis rue Spontini, Paris.
Photograph by Claude Azoulay

H. 1963

ciré
non

Research sketch, autumn–winter 1963
haute couture collection, pencil on paper,
12 1/2 × 4 3/4 in. (32 × 12.5 cm)

Day ensembles from the autumn–winter 1966
haute couture collection.
Photograph by Peter Knapp,
published in Paris *Vogue*

"Line owes its elegance above all to the simplicity and purity of its construction. The line of the body comes before everything. Never overload it, never indulge in too many flights of fancy."

YVES SAINT LAURENT

Formal ensemble worn by Dominique Pommier,
autumn–winter 1969 haute couture collection,
30 bis rue Spontini, Paris.
Photograph by Alexis Witzig

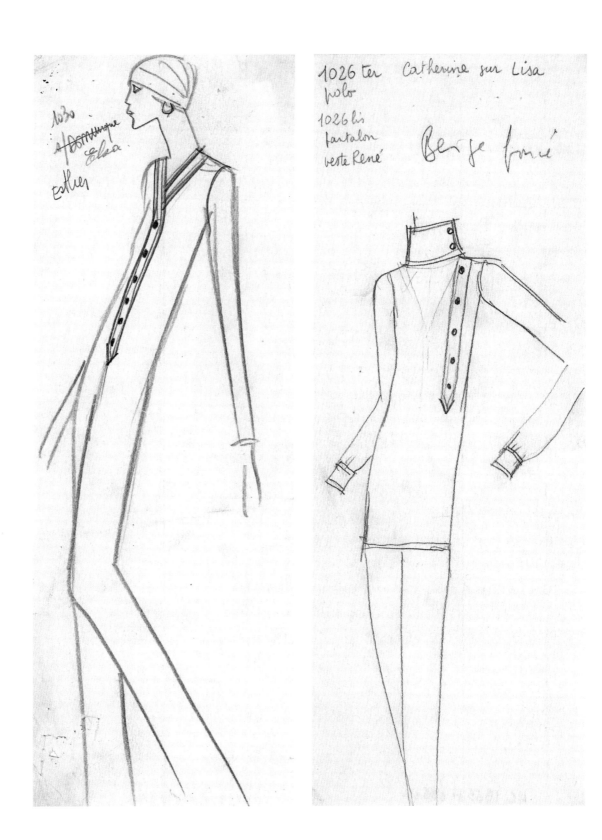

Original sketch for a formal ensemble,
autumn–winter 1969 haute couture collection,
pencil on paper,
12½ × 4¾ in. (32 × 12.5 cm)

Original sketch for a suit,
autumn–winter 1969 haute couture collection,
pencil on paper,
12½ × 4¾ in. (32 × 12.5 cm)

THE SIMPLICITY
OF MATISSE

Yves Saint Laurent and Henri Matisse
(1869–1954) shared a strong attachment
to the Mediterranean, and with it a special love
of color and light. This meeting of minds
was illustrated in their juxtapositions of clear,
bright colors, Matisse in his drawings and
collages and Saint Laurent in his clothes.
Saint Laurent never knew Matisse, but he was
strongly inspired by his work, studying and
admiring his paintings and collages, and
celebrating his art in some of his collections.
It was possibly in 1961, at the exhibition
Grandes gouaches découpées at the Musée
des Arts Décoratifs in Paris, that Yves
Saint Laurent first saw *Le Danseur*, which
he was to purchase with Pierre Bergé in 1982.
The simplicity of the lines and single color
of the dancing figure recall the qualities
that Saint Laurent sought in his jumpsuits.
Using the same economy of means, the
creations of both artist and couturier express
the power of form and color.
M. D.

Henri Matisse, *Le Danseur*, 1937–38,
gouache, graphite, and paper cut-outs on paper,
29¹/₂ × 24¹/₂ in. (74.9 × 62.2 cm),
former Yves Saint Laurent
and Pierre Bergé collection

Georges

Original sketch for a day ensemble,
autumn–winter 1984 haute couture collection,
pencil on paper,
11³/₄ × 8¹/₂ in. (29.5 × 21.5 cm)

Day ensemble worn by Amalia Vairelli,
autumn–winter 1984 haute couture collection.
Photograph by Claus Ohm

JUMPSUITS

At his spring–summer 1975 haute couture
show, Yves Saint Laurent unveiled nine
jumpsuits for day and evening wear
in neutral and monochrome tones. Here
he used wool gabardine for its firm texture,
which emphasizes the rigor of the cut.
His very first haute couture jumpsuit made
its appearance in his spring–summer 1968
collection. It was to become one of his iconic
designs, particularly as he created it in
different variations in so many of his shows.
A feminine reinterpretation of the working
overalls worn by airmen and, later, astronauts,
it was designed to highlight the silhouette
of the body and offer fluidity in movement.
A. C.-S.

SINGIN' IN
THE RAIN

JUMPSUIT SAHARÏENNE

Jumpsuit de gabardine havane de Carlotto, à manches longues, poches plaquées et ceinture de cuir roux. Foulard beige doré, bracelet bois et or. Coiffure Philippe pour Maurice Franck. Tous les modèles sont d'Yves Saint Laurent Haute Couture. Accessoires Saint-Laurent.

SINGIN' IN
THE RAIN

JUMPSUITS VERSION SOIR

A gauche, jumpsuit de jersey de soie ivoire de Racine, à ceinture coulissée et manches longues. Collier jade et jais. Chaussures mordorées.

A droite, jumpsuit smoking de gabardine noire de Carlotto, manches longues, ceinture cuir et vernis noir. Fleur blanche à la poche, bandes de satin sur les côtés du pantalon. Bracelets élastiques jais, strass et or. Boucles d'oreille carrées jais et perles. Chaussures vernies noires. Coiffures Philippe pour Maurice Franck.

Jumpsuits, spring–summer 1975
haute couture collection.
Photographs by Marc Hispard,
published in *Harper's Bazaar*

Research sketch for a jumpsuit,
spring–summer 1975 haute couture collection,
felt pen on paper,
$10^5/_8 \times 8^1/_4$ in. (27 × 21 cm)

Jumpsuit worn by Wong, spring–summer 1975
haute couture collection

BETTY CATROUX,
SPIRIT OF THE AGE

Betty Catroux (b. 1945) met Yves Saint
Laurent in 1967. Her androgynous appearance
fascinated the couturier, for whom she
embodied a feminine ideal. He saw in her
"the spirit of the age," in which fashion was
"a state of mind more than clothes." Before
meeting Saint Laurent, with whom she would
become inseparable friends, Betty Catroux
had already cultivated a taste for men's
clothes, which made her feel fully herself.
With her husband, the interior decorator
François Catroux (1936–2020), she expressed
the same modern spirit in the decoration
of their apartment. This private world was
skillfully enlivened with works by contemporary
artists such as Victor Vasarely (1906–1997),
op artist Luis Tomasello (1915–2014), and
Àngel Duarte (1930–2007). In February 1970,
American *Vogue* described their home
as an "op-art-ment."
A. C.-S.

Betty Catroux wearing Yves Saint Laurent
in her apartment, Paris, 1969.
Photograph by Jeanloup Sieff,
published in Paris *Vogue*

Dress worn by Rebecca Ayoko,
autumn–winter 1985 haute couture collection

Day ensemble worn by Edia Vairelli,
autumn–winter 1984 haute couture collection

Original sketch for a dress,
spring–summer 2001 haute couture collection,
pencil on paper,
11³/₄ × 8¹/₂ in. (29.5 × 21.5 cm)

Dress worn by Bambi, spring–summer 2001
haute couture collection.
Photograph by Guy Marineau

Research sketch, autumn–winter 1963
haute couture collection, pencil on paper,
10$^{1}/_{2}$ × 8$^{1}/_{4}$ in. (26.4 × 20.9 cm)

Ensemble of grosgrain, felt, canvas,
leather, and overstitched hats,
spring–summer haute couture collections,
1980, 1985, 1987, and 1991.
Photograph by Matthieu Lavanchy

"My weapon lies in the way I look at my era
and the art of my era."

YVES SAINT LAURENT, 1990

Formal ensemble worn by Khadija Adam Ismail,
autumn–winter 1988 SAINT LAURENT
rive gauche collection.
Photograph by Roxanne Lowit

PARIS INTERIORS

The décor of Yves Saint Laurent and
Pierre Bergé's apartment at 3 place Vauban
from 1961 to 1970 was studiedly sober
and restrained. Among other pieces,
the furniture included a Knoll table, Barcelona
armchairs by Mies van der Rohe (1886–1969),
and an armchair by Charles and Ray Eames
(1907–1978 and 1912–1988). In 1968,
the couturier declared that he would really
like to "live in a desert … in an empty apartment
with very few things." The decoration of their
new home, on rue de Babylone, was
nonetheless far removed from this pared-back
spirit, which was more evident in Yves
Saint Laurent's studio on avenue de Breteuil.
When he bought this in 1974, he asked the
interior decorator Jacques Grange (b. 1944)
to create a work space with "clean lines"
as in the movies of Michelangelo Antonioni
(1912–2007).
A. C.-S.

Salon of Yves Saint Laurent's apartment
on avenue de Breteuil, Paris, 2008.
Photograph by Ivan Terestchenko

SAINT LAURENT *RIVE GAUCHE*:
A NEW AESTHETIC

In 1966, Yves Saint Laurent decided to
create a ready-to-wear line, SAINT LAURENT
rive gauche, to which he devoted the same
care, attention, and creativity as he did to
his haute couture. He opened his first boutique
at 21 rue de Tournon, in the 6th arrondissement
of Paris, laid out by interior designer Isabelle
Hebey (1935–1996). A new concept, it was
bold, original, and uncompromisingly modern
for its time. The hushed ambience, the warm
reds and oranges, and the geometrical forms
showcased Saint Laurent's designs, notably
presented on double rows of clothes rails.
The space was also punctuated with works
of art: a portrait of Yves Saint Laurent
by Eduardo Arroyo (1937–2018), Djinn benches
by Olivier Mourgue (b. 1939), lamps by
Isamu Noguchi (1904–1988), and sculptures
by Niki de Saint Phalle (1930–2002).
J. L.

The first SAINT LAURENT *rive gauche* boutique,
21 rue de Tournon, Paris, 1966

Yves Saint Laurent

*annonce
l'ouverture
de
son magasin*

SAINT LAURENT
rive gauche

*PARIS
21, rue de Tournon*

Invitation to the opening of the first
SAINT LAURENT *rive gauche* boutique
at 21 rue de Tournon, 1966.
Photograph by Harry Meerson

Catherine Deneuve and Yves Saint Laurent
in the first SAINT LAURENT *rive gauche* boutique,
21 rue de Tournon, Paris,
September 28, 1966.
Photograph by Alain Nogues

Pages 56–57:
Yves Saint Laurent with a model
during the preparations for his first collection
in his own name, 11 rue Jean-Goujon, Paris,
December 1961.
Photograph by Pierre Boulat

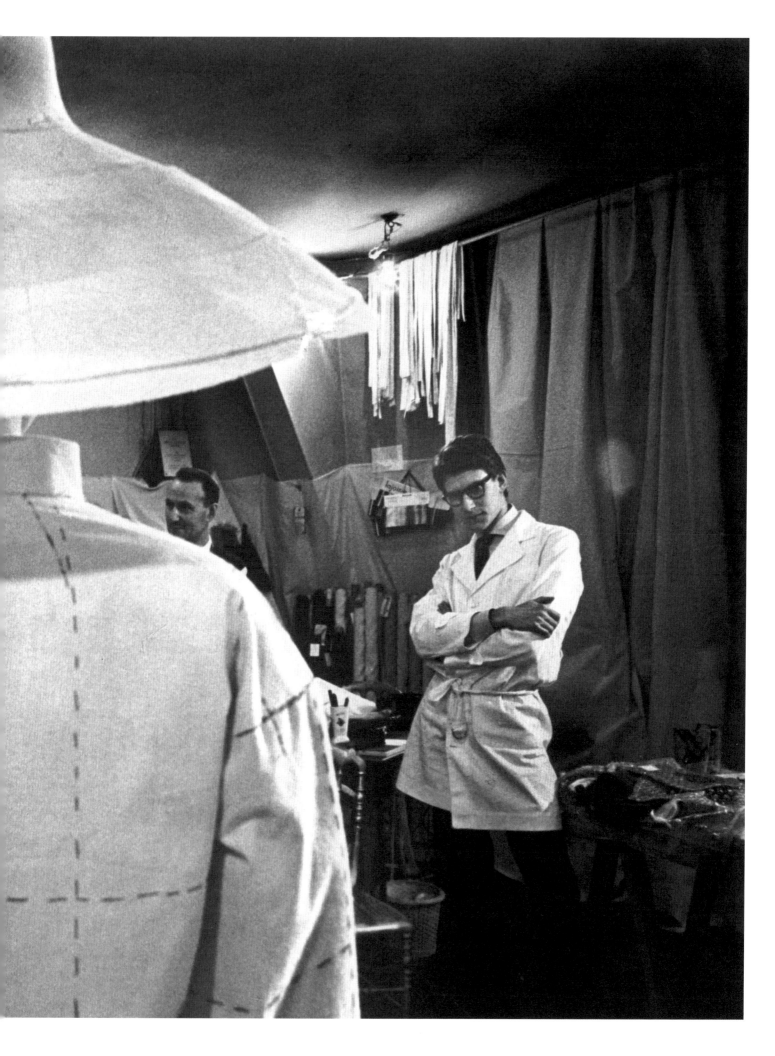

COLORS

"Like fashion, art reflects its times,
and it is only natural that contemporary painting
should influence fashion.
Unless it's the other way round."

YVES SAINT LAURENT, 1990

Page 58:
Yves Saint Laurent at the opening
of his first retrospective exhibition
at the Metropolitan Museum of Art in New York,
December 1983.
Photograph by Roxanne Lowit

Silk satin jacket and hat
from a formal ensemble, autumn–winter 1988
SAINT LAURENT *rive gauche* collection.
Photograph by Matthieu Lavanchy

THE PALETTE OF AN ABSTRACT COUTURIER

SERENA BUCALO-MUSSELY

In his theory of colors, Vassily Kandinsky described the two stages of the experience of looking at a painting: initially, a "purely physical" effect is created by the discovery of new shades; then the "emotional" resonance of colors is felt, referring back to the viewer's education and memories.[1] In this way, the viewer's gaze takes in the harmony of forms and colors on the canvas, which switches between a reading of the composition as a whole and focusing in on the details. In the history of fashion, the greatest designers have been able to translate the medium of painting into the medium of fabric, so offering the same visual experience as the great painters. Through the artistic aspect of his work[2] and also the intensity of his passion for color, Yves Saint Laurent offers one of the most striking examples of this transposition.

For Saint Laurent, color was the medium that enabled him to conceive his designs. Like an artist, he used what he called his "Van Dyck browns," "Veronese greens," "Turner mauves," and "Goya grays" to compose his forms. "It is you who stands before the fabric and color, you who, like a painter with his brushes, like a sculptor with his clay, have to get to grips with the medium,"[3] he explained in an article in *Le Monde* newspaper marking his first retrospective in a museum in 1983. In an essay he wrote in 1993, the historian Michel Pastoureau described the "polyphony" of Saint Laurent's colors, stressing the close links between the garments and their colors, an essential factor in an algebraic formula that also encompassed the design, fabric, shade, cut, and accessories.[4] In Yves Saint Laurent's work, color metamorphosed into form and hence became its own expression.

ABSTRACT FORMS AND POP ART COLORS

Wanting to represent the new liberated woman of the 1960s,[5] at the start of his career, Yves Saint Laurent, like his contemporaries,

1. Wassily Kandinsky, *Du spirituel dans l'art, et dans la peinture en particulier*, ed. Philippe Sers (Paris: Denoël, 1989); published in English as *Concerning the Spiritual in Art*, ed. Adrian Glew, trans. M.T. Sadler (New York: MFA Publications and London: Tate Publishing, 2001).
2. Yves Saint Laurent designed several collections as tributes to artists, including Piet Mondrian and Serge Poliakoff (1965), Georges Braque and Vincent Van Gogh (1988), Henri Matisse (1980 and 1981), Pablo Picasso (1979), and David Hockney (1987).
3. Yves Saint Laurent quoted by Hervé Guibert in "Yves Saint Laurent au Metropolitan," *Le Monde*, December 8, 1983, published to coincide with his exhibition at the Metropolitan Museum of Art, New York.
4. Michel Pastoureau, "Héraldique de la couleur," in *Yves Saint Laurent. Exotismes* (Marseille: Musées de Marseille / Paris, Réunion des musées nationaux, 1993), 47.
5. "When I was given this extraordinarily beautiful book on Mondrian, it seemed to me that with the architecture of their black lines and the brilliance of their colors, Mondrian's paintings could serve as the basis for garments that would show the feminine wardrobe in a new light." Yves Saint Laurent, interview for *Tages-Anzeiger Magazin*, December 20, 1975.

embarked on experiments with different forms, materials, and colors. To do this, he borrowed the visual codes of abstraction and adapted them for use in fabrics. The Dutch De Stijl artist Piet Mondrian, whose work he knew through Michel Seuphor's monograph,[6] inspired his autumn–winter 1965 collection (p. 63). His straight-cut wool jersey dresses were simple and restrained, such that, in an extension of the Bauhaus aesthetic,[7] his outfits appeared practical and comfortable to wear. Veritable "collages" in three dimensions, they were meticulously composed from a grid of black strips with colored rectangles applied within this rectilinear matrix. The arrangement of these "small ceramic tiles"[8] of color lent the designs their form,[9] as Saint Laurent definitively appropriated Mondrian's dictum that "only pure relationships, of pure constructive elements, can produce pure beauty." The autumn–winter 1965 collection also included designs inspired by a more contemporary painter, Serge Poliakoff, one of the leading figures of postwar lyrical abstraction, then at the height of his success. Sharing Poliakoff's preference for expressiveness of color and simplicity of form, Saint Laurent created dresses consisting of irregular, interlocking geometric shapes in strong and contrasting colors (pp. 74–75).

Saint Laurent continued this theme of layering wool jersey in different colors in his autumn–winter 1966 collection, designing jigsaw puzzle dresses in a range of shades evoking the psychedelic trends of pop art.[10] Waves cut from fabrics in bright and sometimes strident shades (turquoise, yellow, orange, fuchsia, green, purple) contrasted with and complemented each other, via sharp transitions and asymmetrical cuts. If an ensemble was black, meanwhile, he would pep it up with touches of acid colors (pp. 76–77). Breaking away from traditional forms and imposing his new style, Saint Laurent thus modernized fashion.[11]

The cocktail dresses in this collection, embellished with a female profile or nude silhouette, referenced the pop artists Jim Dine, Roy Lichtenstein, and Tom Wesselmann (p. 71). The collection was a massive success; the American magazine *Life*[12] gave a double-page spread to it, posing the models against a background of giant matches by Raymond Hains, founder of the *nouveau réalisme* movement (pp. 68–69). Pop art was also a presence in the first SAINT LAURENT *rive gauche* ready-to-wear boutique (pp. 52–53), which opened the same year on rue de Tournon in Paris. The modern décor was enhanced with paintings,[13] and a sculpture by Niki de Saint Phalle was installed in the courtyard on the opening day.[14] A similarly joyous spirit to that of the artist who created the *Nanas* was to be seen in the coat of a wedding ensemble Saint Laurent designed for his 1970 haute couture collection: made up of flat panels in vivid colors, it sported the message "LOVE ME FOR EVER OR NEVER" on both front and back in large velvet and satin letters.

THE SHOCK OF COLOR

From pop art to minimalism, color continued to occupy an important place throughout the 1970s. As in other major world capitals, installations by numerous artists were incorporated

6. Michel Seuphor, *Piet Mondrian. Sa vie, son œuvre* (Paris: Flammarion, 1956).

7. Form follows function.

8. M.-A. Dabadie, "Yves Saint Laurent. Un style bicolore," press cutting from an unidentified newspaper, 1965, Musée Yves Saint Laurent Paris Archives.

9. Interview with Yves Saint Laurent in *Tages-Anzeiger Magazin*, December 20, 1975.

10. An expression of the new consumer society, pop art was popularized by the New York World's Fair in 1964. Works by pop artists (Andy Warhol, Roy Lichtenstein, Jim Dine, and Tom Wesselmann, among others) were popularized in Europe by new galleries such as the space opened by Ileana Sonnabend on quai des Grands-Augustins in Paris in 1962.

11. Interview with Yves Saint Laurent in *Tages-Anzeiger Magazin*, December 20, 1975.

12. "Paris Fall Styles Full of Surprises," with photographs by Jean-Claude Sauer, *Life*, September 2, 1966.

13. Decorated by the designer Verner Panton (1926–1998), the boutique notably featured paper lamps by Isamu Noguchi (1904–1988).

14. A *Nana* from the set for the ballet *Éloge de la folie* (1966) by Roland Petit.

"Homage to Mondrian" cocktail dresses,
autumn–winter 1965 haute couture collection.
Photograph by Joseph Leombruno
and Jack Bodi, published in *Life*

Guy de Rougemont, *Mise en couleurs
d'un musée*, ephemeral project for the
Musée d'Art moderne de la Ville de Paris, 1974

into the urban fabric of Paris.[15] When Yves Saint Laurent moved into his new fashion house at 5 avenue Marceau,[16] he could hardly have missed the polychrome vinyl sheaths that Guy de Rougemont had installed on the columns of the Palais de Tokyo, just a few steps away, in late 1974 (p. 64). Like the books in Saint Laurent's library, new developments in art were a source of inspiration for him in his work.[17] His passion for color was also evident in his choice of reading matter, which included works on Henri Matisse, naturally, as well as the Bauhaus, Paul Klee,[18] and Sonia Delaunay,[19] along with more general works on abstract art.[20] Also in the library were the workbooks and studies of color used by professionals working in fashion and ready-to-wear.[21]

When in the late 1960s Yves Saint Laurent discovered Morocco, and especially its dazzling light,[22] the country opened up the "doors of color" to him.[23] He felt a sense of liberation, and was ready to "get to grips with color"[24] and to use it to compose new forms. His ensembles from this time feature pieces in startling color combinations such as pink and red, pink and orange, purple and red, and green and blue, which almost went "against nature" in the world of couture. Shades in both clothes and accessories were clear and bright, as was seen to particularly striking effect in the autumn–winter collections in 1976 (Opera-Ballets Russes), 1987, 1990, 1992, and 2001.

In suits, the color of the blouse was never the same as the jacket and skirt, while two-tone capes set up a dialogue with evening dresses of different colors. A detail was enough to pep up an ensemble with a bold touch of color in a stole, buttons, hat, gloves, or belt.

In his 1984 haute couture collection (pp. 88–89) and his 1997 ready-to-wear collection (pp. 90–93), Saint Laurent composed his outfits by overlaying broad bands of jersey in solid colors. Parallels between these collections and the formal approach of abstract painters such as Ellsworth Kelly (above) and Aurélie Nemours are striking.[25] Blocks of brilliant flat color came one after another as in a color

spectrum, separated by sharp transitions and clear lines.[26] The shades of color were sublime, and there was no need for Saint Laurent to resort to elaborate forms in order to construct his designs.

All of these influences coalesced in perfect synthesis in the autumn–winter 1988 collection

15. For example, the wall painted by François Morellet on rue Quincampoix in the 3rd arrondissement of Paris.
16. From its original premises at 30 bis rue Spontini, the couture house moved in 1974 to avenue Marceau in the 16th arrondissement of Paris.
17. Yves Saint Laurent, "Saint Laurent raconte trente ans de passion," *Elle*, January 1992.
18. Christian Geelhaar, *Paul Klee et le Bauhaus* (Paris: La Bibliothèque des arts / Neuchâtel: Éditions Ides et calendes, 1972).
19. Jacques Damase, *Sonia Delaunay. Rythmes et couleurs* (Paris: Hermann, 1971).
20. Michel Seuphor, *L'Art abstrait*, vol. 1, *1910–1918. Origines et premiers maîtres* (Paris: Maeght, 1971). Many of the books in Yves Saint Laurent's library were published in the 1970s.
21. Ellen Marx, *The Contrast of Colors* (New York: Van Nostrand Reinhold Company, 1973).
22. With Pierre Bergé he bought a house there: Dar el-Hanch ("The Snake's House").
23. "Interview d'Yves Saint Laurent," *Paris Match*, December 16, 1993.
24. Ibid.
25. Saint Laurent shared an interest in Mondrian's geometrical abstraction with these artists.
26. Saint Laurent had already used line to trace the collar and cuffs of a long double-breasted coat in blue wool gabardine, as well as a jacket tribute to Picasso's *Portrait of Nusch Éluard* (1937), both from the autumn–winter 1979 collection. In the summer of 1988, he used the same colored line in suede suits (pp. 96–97).

65

Ellsworth Kelly, *Red, Yellow, Blue I*, 1963, acrylic on canvas, 7 ft. 6 in. × 7 ft. 6 in. (228.6 × 228.6 cm), Fondation Maeght, Saint-Paul-de-Vence

for SAINT LAURENT *rive gauche* (pp. 104–11). The Cubist skirt suit series consisted of jackets structured by black lines that described shapes and drew diagonals, so highlighting the cut and emphasizing the silhouette. Saint Laurent's paring back of both form and color palette were here seen at their peak, with designs verging on the abstract that created a stained-glass effect. In the age of full sleeves and big bows, Saint Laurent caused universal surprise by creating ensembles that in their construction recalled the geometry of Sonia Delaunay's costumes for Tristan Tzara's *Le Cœur à gaz* (1921)[27] (left), which had already been reprised by David Bowie for his performance of "The Man Who Sold the World" on *Saturday Night Live* in 1979. Saint Laurent chose five designs from this collection for the fashion show mounted at the Fête de l'Humanité in September 1988, when he declared to the journalists present: "Couture is a form of painting and sculpture." And it was true: these jackets were transformed into artists' palettes, genuinely painterly spaces in which arrangements of abstract forms took shape.

With his genius for fashion, Yves Saint Laurent was a master of form and color, with an extraordinary ability to create beautifully structured designs and combinations of bold, vibrant colors. Using unexpected color palettes and juxtapositions of contrasting textures, he created breathtaking pieces and pushed the boundaries of fashion. His pared-back, modern silhouettes formed the cornerstone of a unique style that has endowed the history of art and fashion with an indelible legacy.

27. The play was first performed at the Galerie Montaigne (Studio des Champs-Élysées, Paris) on June 10, 1921. Sonia Delaunay's costume designs were reproduced in *Sonia Delaunay: Rythmes et couleurs* by Jacques Damase (1971), one of the books in Saint Laurent's studio library.

Sonia Delaunay, *Mademoiselle Bouche et Monsieur Œil*, costumes for *Le Cœur à gaz* by Tristan Tzara, 1923, watercolor and pencil on paper, 12¼ × 9 in. (31.2 × 22.8 cm), Museum of Modern Art, New York

Formal ensemble worn by Gurmit Kaur Campbell,
autumn–winter 1988 SAINT LAURENT
rive gauche collection

A POP ART COLLECTION

Several of the dresses in the autumn–
winter 1966 haute couture collection made
reference to American artists contemporary
with Yves Saint Laurent, including
Tom Wesselmann (1931–2004) and Roy
Lichtenstein (1923–1997). The influence
of pop art could be felt in the combinations
of vivid colors and figurative motifs.
For the September 1966 issue of *Life*
magazine, these designs were photographed
by Jean-Claude Sauer (1935–2013) in front
of giant matches by the French artist
Raymond Hains (1926–2005). At the same
time, Hains's work was also on display
at the Iris Clert gallery in Paris, in an exhibition
entitled *Seita et Saffa, copyright by Raymond
Hains*. The dynamic and brilliantly colorful
photographs published in *Life* expressed
all the modernity and imagination of
Yves Saint Laurent's designs, and more
generally of the spirit of the 1960s.
A. C.-S.

Pages 68–69:
"Homage to Pop Art" cocktail dresses,
autumn–winter 1966 haute couture collection.
Photograph by Jean-Claude Sauer,
published in *Life*

"Homage to Tom Wesselmann" evening dress
and cocktail dress in front of a work by Raymond Hains,
autumn–winter 1966 haute couture collection.
Photograph by Jean-Claude Sauer

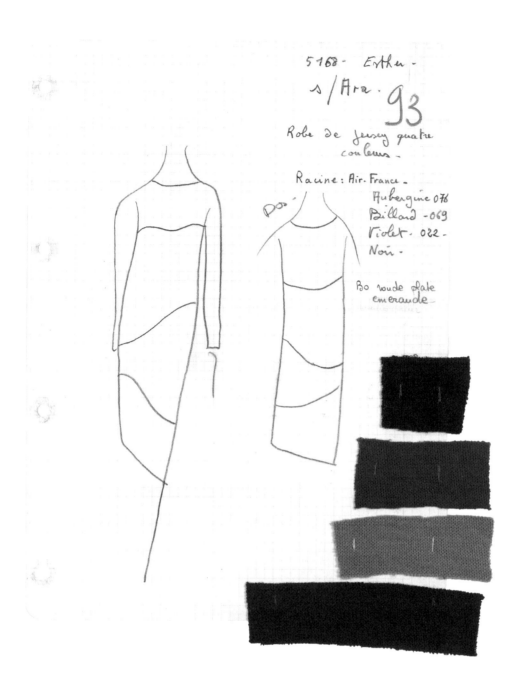

Atelier specification sheet or *feuille de Bible*
("Bible sheet") for a formal dress,
autumn–winter 1966 haute couture collection,
pencil on paper with fabric samples stitched on,
$10^5/_8 \times 8^1/_4$ in. (27 × 21 cm)

Françoise Hardy wearing Yves Saint Laurent
in front of a work by Victor Vasarely, 1967.
Photograph by Patrice Picot,
published in *Jours de France*

HOMAGE
TO SERGE POLIAKOFF

For his autumn–winter 1965 collection,
Yves Saint Laurent borrowed from the work
of one of the great names of modernism,
the abstract painter Serge Poliakoff
(1900–1969), transposing his paintings into
fabrics and composing dresses by
superimposing fields of flat color: bottle green,
eggplant purple, and red. Fabric and color
were subordinate to form: the construction
was very simple, the lines straight and narrow.
As in a Poliakoff painting, the colors brought
the whole design to life, thanks to the skillful
overlaying of pieces of jersey. Saint Laurent
declared: "In my last collection I was inspired
for the first time by Mondrian and Poliakoff,
who I find more interesting for their
architectural side than in their decorative
aspect. . . . Through Poliakoff and Mondrian
I have been rejuvenated and refreshed
in an extraordinary way: they have taught
me purity and balance."
S. B.-M.

"Homage to Serge Poliakoff" cocktail dress
in wool jersey, autumn–winter 1965 haute couture collection.
Photograph by Matthieu Lavanchy

Skirt suit, hat, and gloves in wool jersey,
breitschwantz, and leather,
autumn–winter 1966 haute couture collection.
Photograph by Matthieu Lavanchy

TOWARD ABSTRACTION

The 1966 "Homage to Pop Art" collection
was surprising for the mastery of simple forms
and bright colors that Yves Saint Laurent
displayed. He avoided half-tones and worked
with color as though it was a material, favoring
startling clashes and vibrant contrasts in fields
that were clearly and visibly delineated.
This daywear ensemble consists of a simple
"Trapeze" line jersey dress and two-tone
jacket. Saint Laurent used a vivid color
to pick out the lines of the jacket, the yellow
contrasting sharply with the black background.
He cut directly into the color of the fabric,
like an abstract artist painting a canvas.
This contrasting ensemble was worn with
a fuchsia oilskin coat (pp. 78–79), a fur hat
in a remarkable shape dubbed "Robin Hood"
by Saint Laurent, patent leather boots,
and the most basic of white gloves.
S. B.-M.

Day ensemble worn by Lizzie, autumn–winter 1966
haute couture collection, rue Spontini, Paris.
Contact sheet by Jacques Verroust

Day ensembles from the autumn–winter 1966
haute couture collection.
Photograph by Jean-Louis Guégan,
published in *L'Officiel*

YVES SAINT LAURENT
AND PIET MONDRIAN

The work of Piet Mondrian (1872–1944)
raised many questions for Yves Saint Laurent
and made a profound impression on him.
For his autumn–winter 1965 haute couture
collection, he created twenty-six designs
that echoed the abstract paintings of this
leading figure of neoplasticism. The designs
that caused the greatest sensation were
the cocktail dresses, in which he re-created
Mondrian's large blocks of flat color contained
within thick black lines using squares
and rectangles of jersey stitched together
on the inner face. It was a homage to
which Saint Laurent returned throughout
his career. In his spring–summer 1980
haute couture collection, he reprised this
elegant aesthetic in a skirt suit, emphasizing
the simplicity of the cut, the geometry
of the lines, and the clarity of the primary colors.
In 1997, he presented a new version in his
ready-to-wear collection.
J. L.

"Mondrian" suit worn by Mounia Orosemane,
spring–summer 1980 haute couture collection

"Mondrian is purity, and you can't take purity any further in painting. It is the same purity as that of the Bauhaus. The masterpiece of the twentieth century is a Mondrian."

YVES SAINT LAURENT, 2001

Atelier specification sheet or *feuille de Bible*
("Bible sheet") for a "Mondrian" suit,
spring–summer 1980 haute couture collection,
printed paper glued on paper, pencil annotations,
and fabric samples stitched on,
12¹/₂ × 9¹/₂ in. (32 × 24 cm)

114   2140

Mme Felisa
S/ Amalia
Robe de crêpe jaune
(haut)
velours noir
et crêpe bleu (bas)

Crêpe Abraham
3737 col 80 (bleu)
crêpe jaune :
Tarun 17040 col 402

velours Hurel 15471
        noir

2 manchettes feuilles or (carliol)

BO arlequin émail (gripoix)
jaune/ uge/ vert/ bleu
+ poire jaune

Atelier specification sheet or *feuille de Bible*
("Bible sheet") for an evening dress,
autumn–winter 1979 haute couture collection,
printed paper colored with felt-tip pen and glued
on paper, pencil annotations, and fabric samples
stitched on, 12 1/2 × 9 1/2 in. (32 × 24 cm)

Evening dress worn by Amalia Vairelli,
autumn–winter 1979 haute couture collection

Evening dress worn by Khadija Adam Ismail,
spring–summer 1991 haute couture collection

"No collection is like the previous one,
but the technical approach remains the same.
Usually a fabric is the starting point for me,
because fabric is the essential medium
for the creative process, like stone for a sculptor,
and then, sometimes with a very light sketch as a basis,
I shape just as the sculptor sculpts."

YVES SAINT LAURENT, 1982

jersey

Rose

Noir

*Bleu pâle
ou rose →*

1882
OLIVIA
Catherine

Original sketch for a dress, autumn–winter 1984
haute couture collection, pencil on paper,
11³/₄ × 8¹/₂ in. (29.5 × 21.5 cm)

Dress worn by Olivia, autumn–winter 1984
haute couture collection.
Photograph by Guy Marineau

Dress worn by Natalia Semanova,
autumn–winter 1997 SAINT LAURENT
rive gauche collection

COLOR ON THE RUNWAY

The wool jersey dress is a classic of
Yves Saint Laurent couture. This model, from
the autumn–winter 1997 SAINT LAURENT
rive gauche collection, is divided into three
distinct color blocks, turquoise for the body,
red for the yoke, and blue for the skirt,
while the waist is marked by a navy suede
belt. Loud and sometimes startling color
combinations are inventively contained within
a single outfit, which is completed by a
shocking pink scarf and purple suede gloves.
The collection featured four identical dresses
that presented all the colors of the spectrum.
This model marks the transition between
warm and cool tones, between a dress
in yellow, orange, and brown and another
in purple and pink. The final look was in black
and white, white being a mixture of every color
and black signifying their absence.
O. K.

431

Original sketch for dresses, autumn–winter 1997
SAINT LAURENT *rive gauche* collection,
pencil on paper and fabric samples pinned on,
11³/₄ × 8¹/₂ in. (29.5 × 21.5 cm)

Dresses worn by Nieves Álvarez and Carole Naville,
autumn–winter 1997 SAINT LAURENT *rive gauche* collection.
Photograph by Guy Marineau

Sample sheet, autumn–winter 1987
haute couture collection, fabric samples
pinned on paper, 11³/₈ × 8¹/₄ in. (29 × 21 cm)

Study for a LOVE greetings card, 1988,
pastel on paper, 8$\frac{1}{4}$ × 11$\frac{2}{3}$ in. (21 × 29.7 cm)

4317
JP,

Couleur
des
Boutons

Original sketch for a day ensemble,
autumn–winter 1988 haute couture collection,
pastel and pencil on paper,
11³/₄ × 8¹/₂ in. (29.5 × 21.5 cm)

SADIYA 37.
4317 AH88

Day ensemble worn by Sadiya Guèye,
autumn–winter 1988 haute couture collection,
5 avenue Marceau, Paris.
Polaroid by members of the fashion house staff

Formal ensemble worn by Rebecca Ayoko,
autumn–winter 1983 haute couture collection

Original sketch for a day ensemble,
autumn–winter 1988 haute couture collection,
pastel and pencil on paper,
11³/₄ × 8¹/₂ in. (29.5 × 21.5 cm)

Original sketch for a day ensemble,
autumn–winter 1988 haute couture collection,
pencil and pastel on paper,
11³/₄ × 8¹/₂ in. (29.5 × 21.5 cm)

Gurmit Kaur Campbell and Yves Saint Laurent backstage
at the autumn–winter 1988 SAINT LAURENT *rive gauche* show.
Photograph by François-Marie Banier

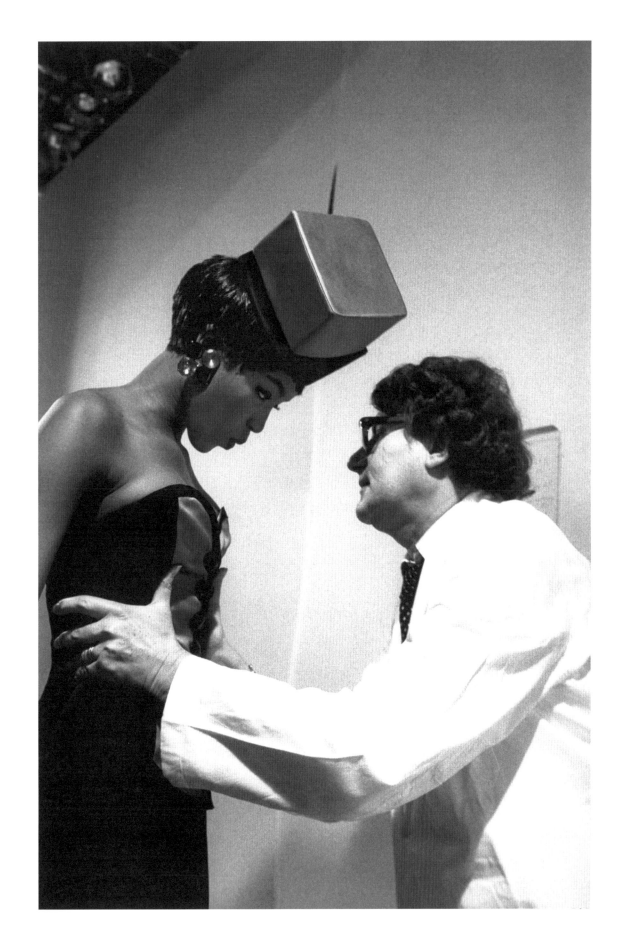

Naomi Campbell and Yves Saint Laurent backstage
at the autumn–winter 1988 SAINT LAURENT *rive gauche* show.
Photograph by François-Marie Banier

AROUND PICASSO

This sketch is one of a series apparently drawn
in a ring-bound sketchbook, as suggested
by the four holes on the top edge of the sheet.
Some thirty of these sketches were inspired
by the work of Pablo Picasso (1881–1973),
and more specifically by the book *Picasso*
by Frank Elgar and Robert Maillard, published
in 1956. Some are annotated "Deauville August
1979," indicating that they were done after
the autumn–winter 1979 haute couture show
a month earlier. That collection paid homage
to the partnership between Serge Diaghilev
(1872–1929) and Picasso for the Ballets Russes.
In this sketch, Yves Saint Laurent reprised in
pastel the geometric motifs in Picasso's *Dancing
Couple*, a watercolor from 1916. Inspired
by the Spanish artist, Saint Laurent played
with volumes and colors to create new forms.
D. E.

Cubist-inspired sketch, 1979, pastel, pencil,
and felt-tip pen on paper,
12$^1/_2$ × 9$^1/_2$ in. (32 × 24 cm)

Original and research sketches,
autumn–winter 1988 SAINT LAURENT *rive gauche* collection,
pencil and pastel on paper,
11³/₄ × 8¹/₂ in. (29.5 × 21.5 cm)

Original and research sketches,
autumn–winter 1988 SAINT LAURENT *rive gauche* collection,
pencil and pastel on paper,
11³/₄ × 8¹/₂ in. (29.5 × 21.5 cm)

INTERLOCKING SHAPES

Inspired by cubism, thirteen jackets from
the autumn–winter 1988 SAINT LAURENT
rive gauche collection were composed from
interlocking geometric shapes cut from
fabrics in contrasting colors. This example
is made from a patchwork of satin cuir—
a fabric that lends the garment a gloss
and firmer structure—in a combination
of five strong and contrasting colors:
pale pink, white, black, fuchsia, and yellow.
The jacket is worn with a black pencil skirt
in satin cuir and accessories that serve
to accentuate the silhouette: a hat fashioned
from two stacked cubes in fuchsia and
black, and earrings made from triangles
and circles. To promote the collection in the
press and other media, Naomi Campbell
was photographed wearing this look by
Arthur Elgort.
D. E.

Formal ensemble worn by Naomi Campbell,
autumn–winter 1988 SAINT LAURENT *rive gauche* collection.
Photograph by Arthur Elgort, published in the campaign catalog

Jacket in silk satin cuir and embroidery
from a formal ensemble, autumn–winter 1988
SAINT LAURENT *rive gauche* collection.
Photograph by Matthieu Lavanchy

Jacket in silk satin cuir and embroidery
from a formal ensemble, autumn–winter 1988
SAINT LAURENT *rive gauche* collection.
Photograph by Matthieu Lavanchy

Formal ensemble worn by Anastasia,
autumn–winter 1988 SAINT LAURENT
rive gauche collection.
Photograph by Xavier Raoux

Pages 110–11:
Backstage at the autumn–winter 1988
SAINT LAURENT *rive gauche* show.
Photograph by François-Marie Banier

BLACK
AND WHITE

"It is a pencil line on a white sheet of paper,
it is a magnificent color."

YVES SAINT LAURENT, 1997

Page 112:
Betty Catroux and Yves Saint Laurent,
New York, September 17, 1968.
Photograph by David Gahr

Dress, hat, and earrings in linen,
grosgrain, cotton, twill, and terracotta,
spring–summer 1983 SAINT LAURENT
rive gauche collection.
Photograph by Matthieu Lavanchy

FROM SCULPTURE
TO MOVEMENT

JULIEN FRONSACQ

Throughout his career, Yves Saint Laurent designed silhouettes in black and white. In liberating himself from pattern and color to focus on line and ensure the design served the silhouette, he became celebrated as the stylist of restraint. Yet, to speak of classicism, asceticism, or minimalism in the context of this couturier who extolled graphic clarity is to fail to do justice to the full scope of his talents. He rethought the lines of garments in movement, and affirmed his place as a creator who was both conceptual and multifaceted in his combinations of artistic disciplines, styles, and genres.

CONTRASTING COLORS
AND MATERIALS

Among the 651 lots in the 2009 auction sale of the collection that Yves Saint Laurent and Pierre Bergé had curated with such care were forty-three paintings, including five by Mondrian, the famous Dutch pioneer of geometric abstraction. The earliest of these was a naturalistic landscape, of which the couple also own a preliminary charcoal drawing. In shades of lilac, the painting depicts a sunset over a river with trees in contre-jour. Together, the Mondrians in Yves Saint Laurent and Pierre Bergé's collection trace the origins of the black grid the artist used to structure his motifs (p. 116). In 1965, this was precisely the system that Saint Laurent

adopted for his autumn–winter haute couture collection (p. 117). In some designs, he divested himself of blocks of primary color to the point of making the grid his sole motif. With the white fur coat in this collection, the elemental reduction of the motif became a form of elegance thanks to the simple addition of black horizontal lines (p. 117 and pp. 132–33).

A passionate lover of painting, Yves Saint Laurent embraced both the radicalism of modern painting and an asceticism that recalls *Portrait of a Man Holding a Book* by Frans Hals, also in Saint Laurent's collection. This painting is a handsome example of the way in which, around 1640, the artist strove to convey dignity and sobriety through the contrast of black and white clothes. Saint Laurent played on the same monochromatic theme, whether in a simple striped jersey dress with fluid lines skimming the body (pp. 136–37 and p. 139), or a satin jacket worn by Jodye (p. 148) with an emphatic shape that set it apart from the transparent top and straight skirt that completed the ensemble.

A collector who possessed both a seventeenth-century Dutch portrait and abstract and geometric paintings was—whether he liked it or not—a man of his time. Yves Saint Laurent was contemporary with the North American trend of the mid-1960s that was then considered "cool" and would later be known as "minimalist." One of the first exhibitions 115

Piet Mondrian, *Ferme sur le Gein, dissimulée par de grands arbres*, 1906–7, charcoal and stump on joined paper, 2 ft. × 3 ft. 1½ in. (61 × 95.4 cm), former collection of Yves Saint Laurent and Pierre Bergé

Piet Mondrian, *Composition with Grid 2*, 1918, reworked by the artist in 1942, oil on canvas, 3 ft. 2 in. × 2 ft. ½ in. (97.4 × 62.5 cm), former collection of Yves Saint Laurent and Pierre Bergé

devoted to this new art trend, held in 1964 and entitled *Black, White, and Gray*, was such a success that *Vogue* used it for a photo shoot. Hence, the first minimalist exhibition was used as a backdrop to promote a new fashion that favored "simplicity" in cuts and volumes and monochrome in color. Dress and motif, background and form, minimalism and baroque were allowed to permeate and penetrate each other, as in stills from *My Fair Lady* (1964) showing Audrey Hepburn dressed in black and white. The following year, *Harper's Bazaar* published a series of portraits of the New York minimalist scene: in Maurice Rentner's photographs, Ellsworth Kelly and Judith Heidler posed in Mollie Parnis, Donald and Julie Judd in Teal Traina, and Paul Thek and Laura Morse in Bill Blass.[1]

In Yves Saint Laurent's work, contrasts were also set up by the unexpected juxtaposition of different materials and motifs. In the white coat from 1965, for example (right and pp. 132–33), glossy black industrial skai® faux leather cinches the noble mink to make it look even more voluminous. Adopting an unorthodox approach, Saint Laurent was a conceptual artist in search of a beauty that was multifaceted, playing with and against a graphic clarity, and always open to every new idea.

GEOMETRY IN MOVEMENT

In the 1950s and 1960s, Paris was the amazing setting for interactions between creative artists in a variety of different fields. In 1955, Denise René mounted a radical exhibition entitled *Le Mouvement*, which introduced new trends in kinetic and op art.[2] Featuring works by Victor Vasarely among others, the show marked a turning point for the Groupe de Recherche d'Art Visuel (GRAV), an artists' collective that explored the heritage of modernism in the present through events featuring viewer participation and the beginnings of interactive forms.[3] This movement towards innovation, interdisciplinary dialogue, and a debunking of the mystique around the forms of modernism extended into the domain of architecture with the creation of the Groupe International d'Architecture Prospective (GIAP).[4] With his "Homage to Mondrian" collection—three years before Brigitte Bardot's robotic intonation of "Contact" in a Scopitone music video in 1968 and one year before the democratization of

1. See James Meyer, *Minimalism: Art and Polemics in the Sixties* (New Haven / London: Yale University Press, 2004).
2. The exhibition *Le Mouvement* was held from April 6–30, 1955, at the Galerie Denise René in Paris.
3. See Frank Popper and Marion Hohlfeldt, *GRAV, Groupe de recherche d'art visuel. Stratégies de participation 1960–1968* (Grenoble: Le Magasin, 1998).
4. The founding manifesto of GIAP was signed in 1965 by critics, architects, and artists including Michel Ragon, Yona Friedman, and Nicolas Schöffer.

Coat from the autumn–winter 1965
haute couture collection.
Photograph by Frederic Scheibe,
published in *Jours de France*

radical fashion in the film *Who Are You, Polly Maggoo?* and GRAV's mobile and interactive sculptures—Yves Saint Laurent emerged as a pioneering figure of transversality. It was while looking at the black tapes that were positioned on dressmakers' mannequins to serve as markers for assembling a garment that he conceived the inspired idea of setting geometry in motion. The head of the *atelier flou* described the moment: "Monsieur Saint Laurent had asked me to make a toile that was completely straight. He put the bolduc tape in place. We were pinning. That was the start of it all."[5] From the moment he showed the collection, Saint Laurent was very clear about his intentions. In appropriating modern abstract painting, he wanted to puncture the mystique of fashion and recall the qualities that were intrinsic to it, such as fluidity and movement: "I realized that we had to stop thinking about clothes as sculpture and look at them instead as something in motion. I realized that up to that point fashion had been stiff, and that from then on it had to be made to move."[6] The simplicity of the ensembles he created in 1978 recalled the fashions of the 1920s that cast off the restrictions of the corset. Yves Saint Laurent designed a straight silhouette that was enhanced by being slightly oversized. In 1994, he added a white line to a black dress to point up the fabric's fluidity and the body's movements, in contrast with the apparent simplicity of the garment (p. 155). The SAINT LAURENT *rive gauche* dress of 1997 was distinguished by the simplicity of its straight, flat cut, the only motif being a white square evoking the masterpieces of the Russian painter Kazimir Malevich (p. 120).

Saint Laurent also rethought the severity of the male wardrobe. For his autumn–winter 1966 haute couture collection, he reprised the type of jacket originally worn by men to smoke their cigars, transforming it into a

5.   Madame Esther, head of the *atelier flou*, quoted by Laurence Benaïm in *Yves Saint Laurent*, rev. ed. (Paris: Grasset, 2002), 229.
6.   Yves Saint Laurent, interview with Patrick Thévenon, *Candide*, August 9, 1965, quoted by Laurence Benaïm in *Yves Saint Laurent*, ibid., 227–28.

Research sketch, autumn–winter 1965
haute couture collection, felt-tip pen on paper,
12 1/2 × 4 7/8 in. (32 × 12.5 cm)

Quilted down jacket in silk satin
from an evening ensemble, autumn–winter 1988
haute couture collection.
Photograph by Matthieu Lavanchy

Kazimir Malevich, *Black Square*, c.1923–30,
oil on plaster, 14$^1/_2$ × 14$^1/_2$ × 3$^1/_2$ in.
(36.7 × 36.7 × 9.2 cm),
Musée national d'art moderne, Paris

radical garment for women—Le Smoking—and signaling a realignment of the poetics of gender (pp. 156–57). In 1966, Saint Laurent designed the costumes for the film *Belle de Jour*, so helping to shape the ambivalent character of its heroine, Séverine Sérizy, a name that evoked at once severity and (in French) the sweetness of cherries. Bourgeois and cold, Séverine, played by Catherine Deneuve, works in a brothel during the day. Influenced by the surrealism of Buñuel, Saint Laurent helped to create an iconic figure who was heir to Madame Bovary and symptomatic of the male gaze. Combining the codes of sexual emancipation with those of entrenched conservatism, Saint Laurent's costumes for the film were a

magnificent blurring of societal and gender norms, and his patent leather pumps, straight skirts, ivory satin collars and cuffs, and trench coat shot to fame. Hollywood had appropriated the military raincoat and turned it into a staple of the female wardrobe; Saint Laurent now designed a black vinyl version with knitted sleeves that was extraordinarily ambiguous and contemporary.

In the 1980s, the rhetoric of postmodernism[7] tried to declare the end of modern history, basing its arguments partly on the question of authorship and revival.[8] Fifteen years earlier, in the mid-1960s, artists had already had recourse to appropriation. Like them, Saint Laurent was inspired by a painter from the past, Mondrian, to transform the grid into a fabric motif. Coming from a generation committed to embracing all the arts, it was not just to painting that Saint Laurent turned his gaze. Throughout his career, he transgressed the fixed boundaries of artistic categories and social norms; similarly, he employed the interplay of black and white to juxtapose the flatness of geometry with the curves and movements of the body. Through fashion, he thus drew inspiration from modern art to drag it out of the hallowed spaces of museums and galleries and make it part of everyday life.

7. Jean Baudrillard, *Simulacres et Simulation* (Paris: Galilée, 1981).
8. Roland Barthes, "La mort de l'auteur," in *Le Bruissement de la langue* (Paris: Éditions du Seuil, 1984); Michel Foucault, *Qu'est-ce qu'un auteur ?* (Paris: Armand Colin, 1970).

121

Jean Tinguely, *White Moving Forms on Black Background (TNT)*, 1957, painted metal, wood, and electric motor, 2 ft. 4³/₈ in. × 2 ft. 1 in. × 9¹/₂ in. (72.1 × 63.5 × 24.1 cm), Solomon R. Guggenheim Museum, New York

Pages 122–23:
Pierre Bergé and Yves Saint Laurent with a model backstage at the spring–summer 1999 haute couture show. Photograph by Derek Hudson

BLACK LINES

All of Yves Saint Laurent's collections
started with a sketch on a blank sheet
of paper, usually in 2B pencil and sometimes
colored with pastels or felt-tip pens.
The lines are clear and precise, showing
no hesitation, and annotations are few
and often added after the sketch was done,
noting production numbers, and names
of ateliers or models. The ateliers would
then interpret each sketch, translating it into
a three-dimensional toile. In some sketches,
Saint Laurent picked out lines in India ink
or black felt pen to add details without
weighing them down with explanations.
In this way, he might specify a fur collar
or sleeves, a strap in a different material,
or an embellishment intended to emphasize
the line of the garment or the shape of
the female body. He might also demonstrate
his thinking more clearly by highlighting
the geometric lines structuring a garment.
D. E.

Research sketch, spring–summer 1963
haute couture collection, ink on paper,
12$\frac{1}{2}$ × 9$\frac{3}{4}$ in. (32 × 24.9 cm)

Research sketch, autumn–winter 1963
haute couture collection, ink on paper,
12$\frac{3}{4}$ × 10 in. (32.4 × 25.4 cm)

Original sketch for a cocktail ensemble,
autumn–winter 1967 haute couture collection,
pencil and felt-tip pen on paper, fabric sample
pinned on, 12$^{1}/_{2}$ × 4$^{7}/_{8}$ in. (32 × 12.5 cm)

Original sketch for a coat, autumn–winter 1969
haute couture collection, pencil and felt-tip pen
on paper, 12¹/₂ × 4⁷/₈ in. (32 × 12.5 cm)

Original sketch for a coat, autumn–winter 1975
haute couture collection, pencil and felt-tip pen
on paper, fabric sample pinned on,
12¹/₂ × 4⁷/₈ in. (32 × 12.5 cm)

"Black is synonymous with line.
And the line is the most important thing.
It is what makes the look."

Yves Saint Laurent drawing on a transparent
sheet with Victoire Doutreleau posing,
rue La Boétie, Paris, 1961.
Photograph by Paul Almasy

Cover photograph of *Vogue Paris Original*,
no. 1556, c.1966

"I am conscious that for many years
I have carried out my work with rigor
and to exacting standards. Making no concessions.
Above all else, I have always respected this profession,
which is not quite an art, but which needs
an artist to exist."

YVES SAINT LAURENT, 2002

PLAYING WITH CONTRASTS

This fur coat from the autumn–winter 1965
haute couture collection typifies the avant-garde
style of the show. Yves Saint Laurent enjoyed
mixing materials and colors—here mink
and faux leather, white and black—to create
strong visual contrasts. This opposition between
white and black, his favorite color, remained
a feature of his creative universe throughout
his career. The apparent simplicity of the design
is lent a fresh dynamic by horizontal lines
that produce optical effects and create
symmetry. Much of Saint Laurent's work was
characterized by graphic design, an important
influence for him: the black line was a form
of expression that was all of a piece with
his unrelenting quest for simplicity and purity.
J. L.

Coat in mink and faux leather and "Belle de Jour" shoes
in patent leather and metal, autumn–winter 1965
haute couture collection. Shoes reproduced for the exhibition
at the Metropolitan Museum of Art in New York in 1983.
Photograph by Matthieu Lavanchy

Formal ensemble worn by Anna de Chambrun,
spring–summer 1973 haute couture collection,
30 bis rue Spontini, Paris

Formal ensemble in silk gabardine and braid,
spring–summer 1973 haute couture collection.
Photograph by Matthieu Lavanchy

Evening ensemble worn by Wong,
spring–summer 1975 haute couture collection

RESTRAINT AND SUPPLENESS

Silk jersey was a strong presence in the spring–summer 1975 haute couture collection, often used in discreet stripes or two-color contrasts. This soft, supple fabric reflected the modern spirit that Saint Laurent wanted to lend his designs. The models in this collection derived their elegance from their pared-back restraint and the way in which they revealed the outlines of the body. The only flight of the imagination in this dress, designed as part of an evening ensemble, was its plunging neckline revealing the back. With this collection, the couturier expressed his desire to create a silhouette that resembled "a line." As his preparatory sketches show, Saint Laurent wanted to simplify the shapes he used in order to stress the verticality of his silhouettes. In an interview for *Tages-Anzeiger Magazin* in 1975, he explained: "Fundamentally I was looking for something that would be like a Brancusi. I wanted something like the vertical metal rays of his 'birds.'"

A. C.-S.

Research sketch, spring–summer 1975
haute couture collection, pencil on paper,
12$\frac{1}{2}$ × 4$\frac{7}{8}$ in (32 × 12.5 cm)

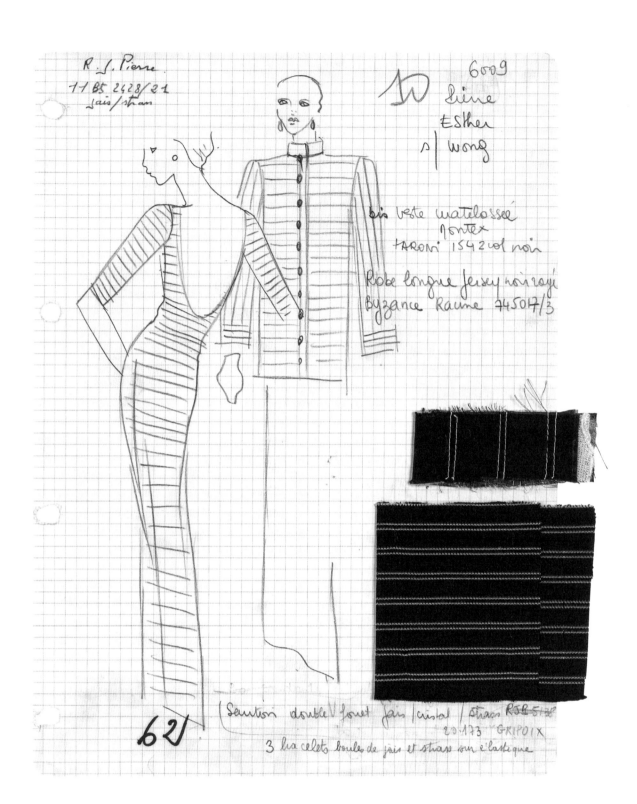

Atelier specification sheet or *feuille de Bible*
("Bible sheet") for an evening ensemble,
spring–summer 1975 haute couture collection,
pencil on paper and fabric samples stitched on,
12½ × 9½ (32 × 24 cm)

TWO-TONE COLLECTIONS

In several of the ensembles in the spring–
summer 1980 SAINT LAURENT *rive gauche*
collection, Yves Saint Laurent chose the
restraint and bold effect of black and white
to play on contrasts and geometric motifs.
In a spirit that was more architectural than
decorative, the couturier designed a series
of models that echoed the parallel aims
of his haute couture creations for autumn-
winter 1979 and spring–summer 1980.
The collection was described by Paris *Vogue*
as "one of the most beautiful" of his ready-
to-wear collections. It shows the legacy
of the inspiration Saint Laurent found when
he first saw Pablo Picasso's designs for
the ballet *Le Tricorne* in 1919. When Mounia
Orosemane wore this skirt suit on the runway,
she was accompanied by Moujik, Saint
Laurent's black-and-white French bulldog.
A. C.-S.

Sketch for a skirt suit, spring–summer 1980
SAINT LAURENT *rive gauche* collection,
pencil and pastel on paper,
19¹/₂ × 13¹/₂ in. (49.5 × 34.3 cm)

Skirt suit worn by Mounia Orosemane
with Yves Saint Laurent's dog, Moujik, spring–summer 1980
SAINT LAURENT *rive gauche* collection.
Photograph by Jean-Luce Huré

Skirt suit, hat, and earrings in braided wool gabardine,
straw, grosgrain, metal, and resin, spring–summer 1980
SAINT LAURENT *rive gauche* collection.
Photograph by Matthieu Lavanchy

Formal ensemble worn by Jerry Hall,
spring–summer 1980 SAINT LAURENT
rive gauche collection.
Photograph by Jean-Luce Huré

Costume design for the "Night and Day"
scene of the variety show *Zizi je t'aime!*
directed by Roland Petit at the Casino de Paris,
1972, gouache and felt-tip pen on paper,
$16^{1}/_{2} \times 11^{3}/_{4}$ in. (41.8 × 29.6 cm)

Ensemble worn by Mounia Orosemane,
spring–summer 1982 haute couture collection

Formal dress worn by Katoucha Niane,
spring–summer 1988 haute couture collection.
Photograph by Claus Ohm

Evening ensemble worn by Jodye Beard,
autumn–winter 1988 haute couture collection.
Photograph by Guy Marineau

EXTRA
HAUTE COUTURE

With this evening ensemble from his autumn–winter 1988 collection, Yves Saint Laurent played with shapes once again and defied the codes of haute couture. Over a silk crepe skirt and a transparent black silk chiffon blouse, he draped a daring *"veste doudounée,"* as he called it on his atelier specification sheet or "Bible sheet," made of black quilted silk satin. With this design a new shape emerged as, like a flower blooming on its stem, the down jacket traced a circular shape above the straight silhouette. A strong contrast is established between the long skirt, the transparent blouse and imposing necklace, and the opaque down jacket, which blurs the shapes and adds a note of cozy comfort to the ensemble.
D. E.

150

Original sketch for an evening dress,
autumn–winter 1981 haute couture collection,
pencil on paper, 12 × 8¹/₄ in. (31 × 21 cm)

Evening dress worn by Nicole Dorier,
autumn–winter 1981 haute couture collection

Evening dress worn by Shiraz Tal,
autumn–winter 1998 haute couture collection.
Photograph by Guy Marineau

153

Evening ensemble worn by Yasmeen Ghauri,
autumn–winter 1994 haute couture collection

Shoes in canvas and suede, spring–summer 1994
SAINT LAURENT *rive gauche* collection

Dress worn by Kate Moss, spring–summer 1994
SAINT LAURENT *rive gauche* collection.
Photograph by Guy Marineau

LE SMOKING

For his autumn–winter 1966 haute couture
collection, Yves Saint Laurent reinterpreted
the smoking jacket that appeared in England
in the 1880s, offering it in a feminine version.
The black of the jacket was deepened
by the grain de poudre wool suiting and
the satin, while the fluidity of the cut created
a silhouette that combined power with
seduction. Although it was not initially
as popular as expected with his haute couture
clientele, in its ready-to-wear version it was
a clear success. Saint Laurent would reprise
this piece throughout his career, adapting it
down the seasons until it became one
of the most iconic examples of his style.
In its most daring versions it was worn over
bare skin.
J. L.

Le Smoking worn by Claudia Schiffer,
autumn–winter 1996 haute couture collection.
Photograph by Guy Marineau

Pages 158–59:
Yves Saint Laurent and models backstage
at the autumn–winter 1983 SAINT LAURENT
rive gauche show.
Photograph by François-Marie Banier

Shoes in patent leather, spring–summer 1979
haute couture collection / spring–summer 1983
SAINT LAURENT *rive gauche* collection.
Composition by Claudia Wieser, 2023

CLAUDIA WIESER

ELSA JANSSEN

The German artist Claudia Wieser makes a regular practice of breaking down the classic boundaries between the fine arts and craft, fashion, and design. The spaces and geometric shapes she constructs using clean lines and interplays of colors and contrasts lend themselves particularly well to setting up a dialogue with the most radical and minimalist of Yves Saint Laurent's creations.

For the exhibition *Yves Saint Laurent: Shapes and Forms* at the Musée Yves Saint Laurent Paris, Claudia Wieser has given free rein to her imagination, devising works that resonate with Saint Laurent's outfits and accessories, using complementary colors, juxtaposed shapes, and contrasting textures. Earthenware tiles, prints on paper, and sculptures in wood create responses to jersey in flat colors, compositions of cotton and silk satin, and mink striped with vinyl.

Starting from preparatory maquettes, Wieser creates an architectural and chromatic space to showcase each of the revolutionary silhouettes by Saint Laurent that have been selected for this exhibition.

In Claudia Wieser's settings, every element finds its own defined place: each of Saint Laurent's creations is enhanced by a network of correspondences between his work in textiles and straight lines, curves, squares, circles, and triangles set within spheres, cones, and cubes.

This fruitful dialogue between the two artists' works continues in the exhibition vitrines that hold displays of accessories. For the exhibition catalog, Claudia Wieser has conceived a new series of compositions. Saint Laurent's bracelets, hats, and hairpins take on the stature of sculptures that verge on abstraction, even to the point of forgetting their original purpose.

Setting Yves Saint Laurent's work in the context of contemporary creativity thus further highlights its artistic dimension.

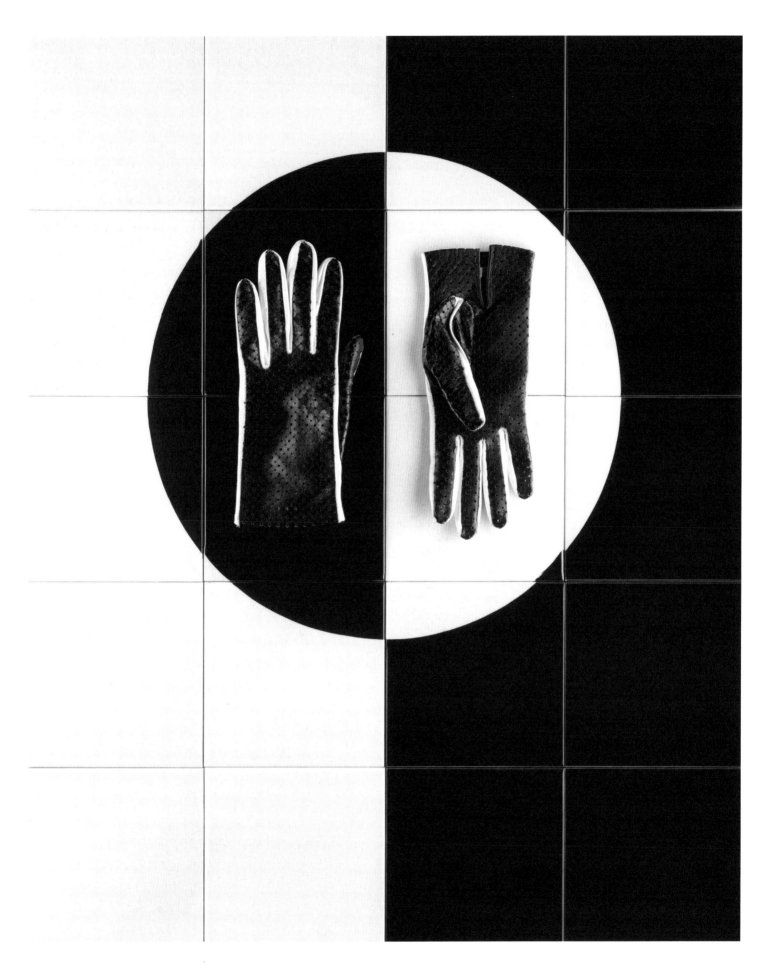

Pair of leather gloves, spring–summer 1983
SAINT LAURENT *rive gauche* collection.
Composition by Claudia Wieser, 2023

Earrings in plastic, terracotta, and ceramic,
spring–summer and autumn–winter 1983
SAINT LAURENT *rive gauche* collections.
Composition by Claudia Wieser, 2023

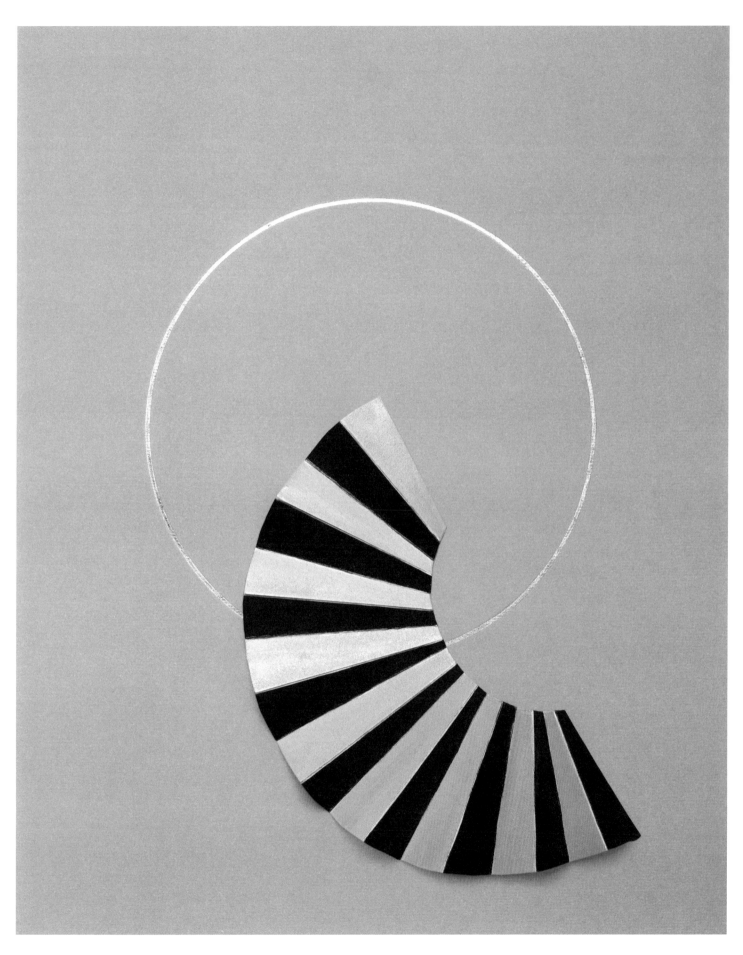

Hair comb in straw, paper, and metal,
spring–summer 1980 SAINT LAURENT
rive gauche collection.
Composition by Claudia Wieser, 2023

Hair comb and bracelets in plastic, resin, and stone,
spring–summer 1980 SAINT LAURENT
rive gauche collection / spring–summer 1982
and autumn–winter 1984 haute couture collections.
Composition by Claudia Wieser, 2023

Clutch bag in cotton and leather, c.1970,
unidentified SAINT LAURENT *rive gauche* collection.
Composition by Claudia Wieser, 2023

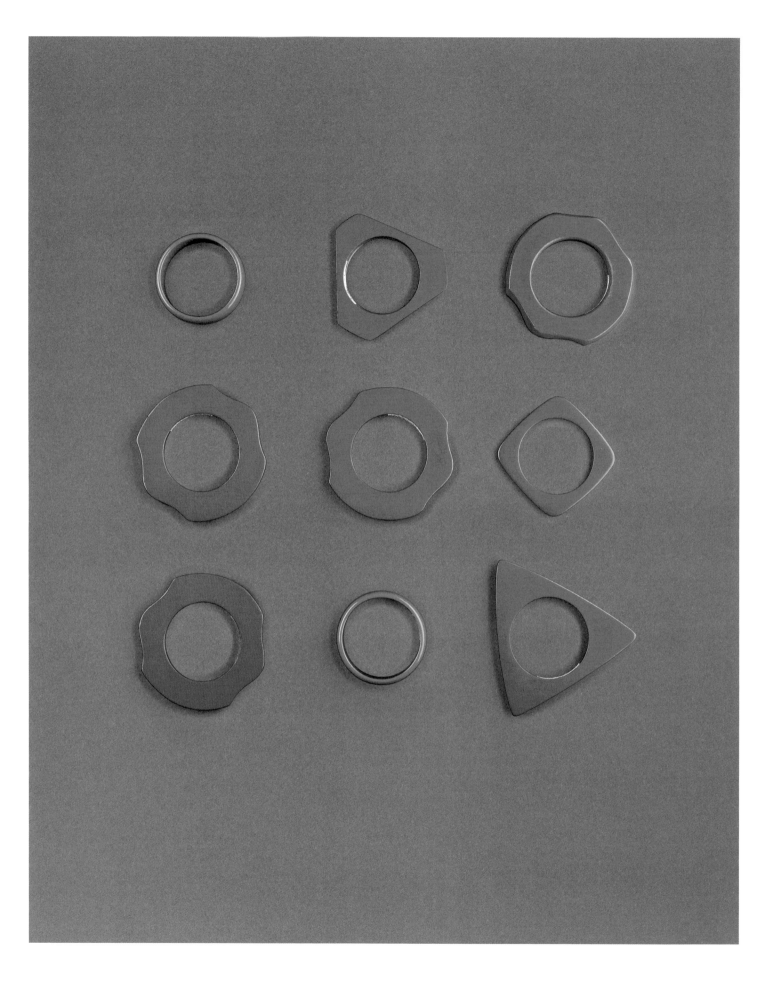

Ensemble of bracelets in plastic,
spring–summer 1967 haute couture collection.
Composition by Claudia Wieser, 2023

Hats in silk satin, autumn–winter 1988
SAINT LAURENT *rive gauche* collection.
Composition by Claudia Wieser, 2023

Bag in suede, autumn–winter 1984
haute couture collection.
Composition by Claudia Wieser, 2023

This book is published to accompany the exhibition *Yves Saint Laurent: Shapes and Forms. Décors and Works by Claudia Wieser*, held at the Musée Yves Saint Laurent Paris from June 9, 2023 to January 14, 2024.

The project has been supported in its entirety by the Fondation Pierre Bergé – Yves Saint Laurent, under its President, Madison Cox.

Unless otherwise stated, the designs displayed in the exhibition are part of the unique heritage of Yves Saint Laurent and Pierre Bergé on the closure of the haute couture house in 2002, which is conserved and promoted by the Fondation in its official role as an organization serving the public interest.

EXHIBITION

HEAD CURATORS

Elsa Janssen
    Director of the Musée
    Yves Saint Laurent Paris

Serena Bucalo-Mussely
    Curator, Head of Collections
    at the Musée Yves Saint Laurent
    Paris

CURATORIAL TEAM

Alice Coulon-Saillard
    Curator, Manager of the
    Photographic, Audio-visual,
    and Press Collections

Domitille Éblé
    Curator, Manager of the
    Graphic Art Collections

Judith Lamas
    Curator, Manager of the Textiles
    and Accessories Collections

GUEST ARTIST

Claudia Wieser

EXHIBITION DESIGN

Agence PAM
    Layout

Élodie Salatko, A.C.L / Transpalux
    Lighting

Charlotte Sobral Pinto
    Graphic Design

FONDATION PIERRE BERGÉ – YVES SAINT LAURENT

MUSÉE
YVES SAINT LAURENT
PARIS

Madison Cox
President

DIRECTION

Elsa Janssen
Director

Laurent Gardette
Administrative and Financial
Director

Marie Delas
Project Manager

CURATORIAL TEAM

Serena Bucalo-Mussely
Curator, Head of Collections

Alice Coulon-Saillard
Curator, Manager of the
Photographic, Audio-visual,
and Press Collections

Domitille Éblé
Curator, Manager of the
Graphic Art Collections

Judith Lamas
Curator, Manager of the Textiles
and Accessories Collections

Clémentine Cuinet
Inventory Manager

Olivia Klusiewicz
Inventory Manager

Jeanne Guy, Lysa Afonso
Interns

EXHIBITION PRODUCTION
AND COLLECTIONS CARE

Tiphanie Musset
Head of Exhibition Production
and Collections Care

Nora Evain-Bentayeb
Manager of Exhibition
Production and Collections Care

Léa Denys
Assistant of Exhibition
Production and Collections Care

Mariana Pagola
Intern

COMMUNICATIONS
AND PUBLIC RELATIONS

Claire Schillinger
Head of Communications
and Public Relations

Giulia Baldini
Manager of Public Relations

Romane Lair
Communications Assistant

Ilana Bret
Intern

ADMINISTRATIVE
DEPARTMENTS

Bénédicte Segré
Administrative and Accounting
Manager

Olivier Chauffeton
General Services Attaché

Maria Ribeiro
Administrative Attaché

Oliver Paulhac
IT Manager

CATALOG

MUSÉE YVES
SAINT LAURENT PARIS

Elsa Janssen
Editorial Direction

Marie Delas
Editorial Coordination

AUTHORS

Cécile Bargues,
Art Historian, Resident
at the National Institute
of Art History (specialized
in twentieth-century art)

Serena Bucalo-Mussely
Curator, Head of Collections
at the Musée Yves Saint Laurent
Paris

Julien Fronsacq
Chief Curator, Deputy Director,
MAMCO, Geneva

LABELS AND
ICONOGRAPHIC RESEARCH

Serena Bucalo-Mussely (S. B.-M.)
Alice Coulon-Saillard (A. C.-S.)
Clémentine Cuinet (C. C.)
Marie Delas (M. D.)
Domitille Éblé (D. E.)
Olivia Klusiewicz (O. K.)
Judith Lamas (J. L.)

STILL LIFES

Matthieu Lavanchy
Photographer

Valérie Weill
Set Designer

COMPOSITIONS

Claudia Wieser
Artist

Thibaut Voisin
Photographer

FLAMMARION

French Edition

Julie Rouart
Editorial Director

Delphine Montagne
Editorial Administration
Manager

Mélanie Puchault
Editor
Assisted by Adèle Ehlinger

Marie-Catherine Audet
Picture Research

English Edition

Kate Mascaro
Editorial Director

Helen Adedotun
Editor

Sarah Rozelle
Editorial Coordinator

Barbara Mellor
Translation from the French

Marie Pellaton
Design and Typesetting

Audrey Sednaoui
Cover Design

Lindsay Porter
Copyediting and Proofreading

Corinne Trovarelli
Production

Les Caméléons
Color Separation

ACKNOWLEDGMENTS

In the context of the exhibition
and catalog *Yves Saint Laurent:
Shapes and Forms. Décors and Works
by Claudia Wieser,* we would like
to express our special thanks to:

Claudia Wieser, both for her
enthusiastic acceptance of our
invitation and for her commitment
and tireless work on the project,
together with Viola Eickmeier
(Studio Violet), her assistants
Mark Emblem and Erika Krause,
her gallerists Nina Höke,
Alexander Sies, Tine Lurati
(Sies+Höke, Düsseldorf),
and Stefan von Bartha (von Bartha,
Basel); Ida Ribbecket, and
Patrick Hutsch;

Céline Bassoul and the House
of Saint Laurent for their loans;

Cécile Bargues and Julien Fronsacq,
who both proposed studies of
Yves Saint Laurent's work in relation
to the artistic movements of
the twentieth century;

Valérie Weill and Matthieu
Lavanchy for their insights into
the pieces on display;

Dominique Deroche and
Clara Saint for their memories and
their involvement; Olivier Châtenet
for his many discussions with
the teams;

Iman Abdulmajid Bowie for
agreeing to allow her image to be
associated with the exhibition,
and her agents Sian Steele
and Tori Edwards;

Jerry Hall, for her kind permission
to use her image on the front cover
of the English edition, and her agent
Tori Edwards;

Guy Marineau, Jean-Luce Huré,
and Arthur Elgort for their
photographs immortalizing
Yves Saint Laurent's creations,
an invaluable source of information
and delight, and for their regular,
faithful, and flexible collaboration
with the museum;

Maxime Catroux and Annie Dufour,
Grégoire Gauger and Claire Simonin
for their advice.

We would also like to offer our
grateful thanks to all the individuals
and partners involved in these
projects alongside the teams of
the Musée Yves Saint Laurent Paris.

Once again, we would like to express
our gratitude to Madison Cox,
President of the Fondation
Pierre Bergé – Yves Saint Laurent,
for the confidence he has placed
in this project.

PHOTOGRAPHIC CREDITS AND COPYRIGHTS

Front cover:
Formal ensemble worn by Jerry Hall,
spring–summer 1980 SAINT LAURENT
rive gauche collection.
Photograph by Jean-Luce Huré

This book is typeset in Dante and Helvetica Neue,
and is printed on Arena Smooth Natural 140 g paper.

Copublished by the Musée Yves Saint Laurent Paris
and Éditions Flammarion, S.A.
Originally published in French as
Yves Saint Laurent – L'Art de la forme
© Éditions Flammarion, S.A., Paris, 2023
© Musée Yves Saint Laurent Paris, 2023

English-language edition
© Éditions Flammarion, S.A., Paris, 2023
© Musée Yves Saint Laurent Paris, 2023

editions.flammarion.com
@flammarioninternational

23 24 25   3 2 1

ISBN: 978-2-08-043052-6
Legal Deposit: 09/2023

Printed in Barcelona, Spain, by Indice